THE
FIFTEEN
PERCENT

THE
FIFTEEN
PERCENT

THE FIFTEEN PERCENT

Overcoming Hardships and Achieving Lasting Success

TERRY GILES

Foreword by
DR. BEN CARSON

Skyhorse Publishing

Skyhorse Publishing books may be purchased in bulk at special discounts for sales promotion, corporate gifts, fund-raising, or educational purposes. Special editions can also be created to specifications. For details, contact the Special Sales Department, Skyhorse Publishing, 307 West 36th Street, 11th Floor, New York, NY 10018 or info@skyhorsepublishing.com.

Skyhorse® and Skyhorse Publishing® are registered trademarks of Skyhorse Publishing, Inc.®, a Delaware corporation.

Visit our website at www.skyhorsepublishing.com.

10 9 8 7 6 5 4 3 2 1

Library of Congress Cataloging-in-Publication Data is available on file.

Cover design by Brian Peterson

Print ISBN: 978-1-5107-5833-9
Ebook ISBN: 978-1-5107-5872-8

Printed in the United States of America

To the two most important ladies in my life: My incredible Mom, LaDon Giles Hix, who helped make me who I am and continues to be my guardian angel; and my wife, Kalli O'Malley, the most remarkable person I have ever met, who makes me better than I could ever be on my own and has brought the gifts of Lauren and Keller into my life.

Contents

Foreword

By Dr. Ben Carson

America is a great place to live in, even if, like Terry Giles, you grew up on the wrong side of the tracks. In this book, Terry examines and expands upon the principles that lead to success in whatever endeavor one embarks upon.

I first met Terry a quarter of a century ago when we were both inducted at a very young age into the Horatio Alger Society of Distinguished Americans. Many decades ago, Horatio Alger wrote many accounts about the lives of Americans who had "rags-to-riches" stories. He was such an influential writer that his works contributed to the establishment of the "American Dream."

In *The Fifteen Percent,* Terry uses many examples from his own very successful legal and business careers in which he created many businesses and opportunities for others, to show the reader that attitude, determination, vision, and hard work are invaluable assets for those who refuse to accept failure. He also shows us how fear of failure can be a cause for failure. Even circumstances that seem to scream "failure" are not always as bad as they seem and, as Terry makes clear, are only part of the puzzle that can eventually manifest over-whelming success.

I can remember times in my surgical career when I was very disappointed with a surgical outcome, but the undesirable outcome led to subsequent success. One such example occurred in 1994, when we attempted to separate conjoined twins in South Africa. The operation was being done under considerably less than optimal conditions, but a fabulous team had been assembled and state-of-the-art equipment and techniques had been imported. It turns out that the twins were symbiotic; one had the kidney function for both, and the other had the heart function for both. We successfully separated them, but the one with no heart function died immediately and the one with no kidney function died days later. Nevertheless, three years later, a set of conjoined twins from Zambia benefited greatly from the previous preparations, and we were able—at the same medical facility—to achieve the first completely successful separation of complexly joined craniopagus twins. They have now finished high school. It would not have happened without the lessons learned in the prior failure. These are the kinds of lessons that Terry repeatedly teaches us in this unique and fascinating book that can empower the reader to define the goal and remain focused on it until it is achieved and then use that success to create the foundation for the next achievement.

The steps can then be repeated endlessly to create a predictable pattern of success. We all can achieve great things, but we must realize that the person who has the most to do with our success is us. Not the circumstances and not other people, but *us*!

—Benjamin S. Carson Sr., M.D.
Professor Emeritus of Neurosurgery, Oncology,
Plastic Surgery, and Pediatrics
Johns Hopkins Medicine

Introduction

A decade or so ago, I served as a lead trial attorney in one of the major sex abuse actions against the Catholic Church. If this sounds grim, it mostly was. Since we had 150 clients (of California's total of eight hundred), it took several months to work through their voluminous case histories, and eight years to resolve the cases. It was a slog through the lowest depths of human depravity. The particulars of what our clients endured as children were gruesome beyond anything reported in the media, and as morally reprehensible as anything I'd experienced, though I'd represented some of the nation's most notorious murderers. Indeed, as I read on, it was clear that the very term "adult survivor" was misplaced. In case after case, these individuals were victims of what psychologist Leonard Shengold terms, with pitiless accuracy, "soul murder."

The one-on-one meetings only added the human dimension to the grim statistics. Even now, in their twenties, thirties, and forties, having to relive those experiences was for most sheer torment. If not etched on their faces the moment they walked through the door, it soon showed itself in sullen silences, out-of-nowhere bursts of anger, or simply cold defiance. It was ever-present, inescapable. Though we were their allies, we were also authority figures, and if there was one lesson burned into their psyches, it was *never* to trust one of those—not a teacher, a cop, a boss, a lawyer, certainly not a priest.

Little wonder that so many had severe drug or alcohol problems, failed in school, or spent time behind bars. What most of us take as the standard markers of normalcy—holding a job, sustaining a relationship, a spouse, a family—were impossibly beyond reach. Their lives as functional human beings had been stopped dead by those long-ago horrors. Even the slightest frustration was an insurmountable object to forward movement. For some clients, this case became their life; they called every day. Three of them would commit suicide before we eventually won.

Yet—and this is the telling thing—a handful among them, perhaps twenty of the 150, stood apart. Not only had they not surrendered to the past, but in surmounting it they discovered a sense of their own power and possibility.

Indeed, early on in the deposition process, I had one of the most memorable encounters of my professional life.

The abuse this particular client had endured was as unspeakably vile as any of the rest. It was all there in his file. He was nine when his father died unexpectedly, the priest presiding over the funeral service afterward seized the opportunity to volunteer himself to the stricken widow as a surrogate father figure for the boy, and the predator was gratefully welcomed into the family home. While the mother cooked dinner, the honored guest would be upstairs molesting her child. It went on for three years. Yet today, in his early forties, he had a postgraduate degree from a highly regarded university; was senior vice president at a prominent San Diego–based electronics company, pulling down more than six figures a year; had been married to the same woman for eighteen years; had two well-adjusted kids, one of whom he coached in little league; and was active in an array of good causes in his community.

He showed up on time for his interview, arriving from work in a well-tailored suit.

"So," he said, during preparation, "what do you want to know?"

I explained that we had what we believed was a pretty complete report, but it would be useful to hear it in his own words.

"That's what I figured," he said with a pained smile. He hesitated a moment, took a deep breath, and launched into it. He spoke for a good half hour, answering my questions along the way, leaving out nothing and adding a number of details I hadn't been aware of. His voice steady, looking me in the eye, he might almost have been discussing someone else.

"You don't seem to have trouble talking about it," I observed.

"Well, I know you have a job to do. I hate what happened, if that's what you're asking, *hated* it. But that was—what?— twenty-eight years ago."

He described the life he'd built for himself, his pride in his professional success and his family.

"How much do your kids know about what happened?"

"Enough—not the details. What they know is the most important thing: bad things happen to everyone, sometimes awful things. The question is whether you let those things define you."

In fact, he had a hard time grasping why so many of the others had been unable to move past it. "Their past has such a hold on them," he noted, with equal parts bafflement and empathy, "they sometimes see people like me as a traitor."

As their lawyer, I could see their point—talk about an ideal witness for the other side, a sure damages killer! But even as I made a mental note to *never* let him near the witness stand, it was impossible not to be struck by his lack of bitterness; and, even more, by his clear sense of its corrosive power.

"Look," he added, as if reading my thoughts, "I don't mean to sugarcoat this. It was bad. It made me feel pretty lousy about myself, it turned me off to organized religion. The only time I enter a church these days is for a wedding or a funeral. My wife's the one who takes the kids to Sunday school."

"But it's okay with you that they go?"

"Listen," he said, "I'm basically a spiritual person. I'm just someone who had bad luck."

Though few articulated it so precisely, it was an attitude shared by every one of the others in that 15 percent who'd gone on to live stable, productive, meaningful lives. They had plans and goals, and surrendering to that awful childhood ordeal was simply not an option. To the extent the experience marked them—and of course it had to—it was in forcing them to harness the emotional resources to surmount it. It made them stronger.

Nor, it turned out, was that 15 percent figure random. Psychiatrists told us that more or less the same percentages applied to other abuse cases across the board—abuse by parent, police officer, teacher, any authority figure. For 85 percent, it destroys their lives. For 15 percent, they not only overcome it, they are stronger because of it.

In his best-selling *David and Goliath,* Malcolm Gladwell surmised that "one time out of ten, out of despair rises an indomitable force." I'm not only an admirer of Gladwell, but a bit more of an optimist. My premise is that the actual number is one and a *half* out of ten—or 15 percent.

Indeed, around the same time, I was seeing very much the same phenomenon in other settings. The greatest honor I've ever received is membership in the Horatio Alger Association of Distinguished Americans, a virtual who's who of American success, and as the society's representative on the scholarship committee, the largest need-based scholarship program in the country, we were awarding tens of millions of dollars a year in scholarships to seriously deprived kids. The candidates were in their midteens and had suffered through often intense adversity. Under the leadership of our extraordinary managing director, Terry Giroux, the Horatio Alger Association now has tens of thousands of applications for 2,500 scholarships. Since we are also looking for young men and women who will not just complete their schooling, but go on to help make the world a better place, Terry organized a panel of psychological experts to help us better evaluate candidates. In their characterization of those apt to keep moving forward regardless of handicaps or barriers, those experts, too, cited the figure of 15 percent. Quite simply, in such cases, fundamental aspects of their makeup dictate that *nothing* will stop them.

What's especially striking, looking closely, is they're very much the same qualities evident among the membership of the Horatio Alger Association itself. As the name suggests, almost all of the members, past and present, are rags-to-riches stories. None of us was predestined for success. Yet from A— baseball's Hank Aaron—to Z—Eastern European immigrant and legendary Paramount Pictures founder Adolph Zukor— each of us came to excel in his or her chosen field; and, indeed, in the words of the organization's charter, to epitomize "the simple but powerful belief that hard work, honesty and determination can conquer all obstacles."

In my case, my professional life has been a series of headlong charges down different paths, some of them simultaneous.

Beginning by building one of California's most successful criminal law firms, I went on, as an entrepreneur, to start and/or buy thirty-five companies, including a car dealership, a bank, and luxury European hotels. Along the way, I produced a play on Broadway, owned magic clubs, and served as a special adviser to or troubleshooter for, among others, Richard Pryor, Werner Erhard, and the children of Martin Luther King Jr.

Looking back, I sometimes still wonder how I got here. Admitted to the Horatio Alger Association in 1994, at the time the third-youngest member (after Oprah Winfrey and Ben Carson), a couple of years later I found myself in a hotel bar at the annual gathering surrounded by John W. Rollins, the business mogul who was educated in a one-room schoolhouse in Georgia, became the man of his household at twelve years of age, and went on to found nine New York Stock Exchange companies; Harry Merlo, the Italian immigrant's son who made his fortune in timber and became one of the Northwest's leading philanthropists; and W. W. "Foots" Clements, a Texas entrepreneurial genius who went from driving a delivery truck to becoming the chairman and CEO of Dr Pepper. I was wide-eyed to be in such august company. They started arguing about who started out the poorest. John Rollins seemed to have been the winner as he related the difficulties of being a dirt farmer in rural Georgia in the 1930s, but Harry raised his hand for the final word. "Lemme tell you guys, we were so poor that on Christmas Eve, Dad would take us out and show us Santa's grave!"

In fact, as we shall see, I could have given Harry a run for his lack of money—at least his father was around, and presumably upright.

What are the qualities and habits of mind that define the 15 percent? Ambition, of course, and drive. But it is more than that. In dealing with those who'd surmounted sex abuse and those who excelled, despite severe adversity, among the young scholarship applicants, it became obvious that they'd have succeeded under *any* circumstances; that if instead they'd suffered severe physical trauma, left paralyzed and wheelchair-bound in an accident, they'd have seen that, too, as a mere impediment, and gone on to live the lives they imagined for themselves.

In history and popular culture, we tend to lionize such people—FDR, Stephen Hawking, Charles Krauthammer, Texas governor Greg Abbott—as of course we should. But what's less evident is that those with the same attributes exist in every realm and field of endeavor. They're the ones who inexorably rise to the top, no matter how they start out or the obstacles they face along the way.

I have long made a point of being on the lookout for such people, both because they're the ones I want to be associated with professionally (success breeding success) and because, this being a rough-and-tumble world, they're often the ones with whom I have to contend.

Take, for instance, Dave Carter.

Not to be immodest, but back when I was a young criminal defense attorney in Orange County, California, I considered myself the fastest gun in the West—until I ran into Dave Carter.

Talk about the 15 percent, this was a guy who let *nothing* stop him. A former track star at UCLA, he was with the marines in Vietnam when his unit was overrun during the battle of Khe Sanh. Badly wounded, having taken twelve or thirteen bullets, he woke up to find the Viet Cong shooting the survivors but managed to crawl into a ravine and hide. It was three days before he was rescued, and he spent three years in the hospital recovering. I mean, one tough SOB.

It was my bad luck that when he was well enough, he went to law school and ended up in the DA's office in Orange County. Let's put it this way: at one point, I won thirty-four criminal cases in a row—mostly acquittals, a couple of hung juries, a handful reduced from first-degree murder all the way down to manslaughter. But that streak was bookended by losses to Dave Carter.

Another of that ilk, a close friend of a friend, is a guy on Long Island named Jerry Kane, who came from the sort of grinding poverty and early scrapes with the law that might easily have led to a life behind bars. Yet instead he wound up a New York State Teacher of the Year, with two generations of ex-students crediting him with their success. "It was his incredible government class that turned me onto politics," as then–Suffolk County Executive Steve Levy joked to the daily *Newsday*. "If people don't like me, they have Jerry Kane to blame." But what's truly extraordinary is that even as Kane was carrying a full teaching load, he was carving out a second, hugely successful career as a builder of luxury homes two hours away in the Hamptons. Now eighty-five and still at it, he muses: "I suppose the other teachers were both jealous and confused, since I was the only millionaire teacher they knew. They didn't seem to get that *anyone* can do it—you just have to work at it."

But of course, those other teachers, among most others, must surely have wondered: Is it really that simple?

Therein lies the real issue: Are the qualities that set such a person apart, that distinguish the 15 percent, innate or learned?

Are a lucky few just *built* that way? Maybe. After all, as every smart advertising executive will tell you, most people are born followers (and only like to think they're not). In contrast, the 15 percent are oblivious to groupthink almost by definition.

However, I also know—and again my own experience is proof—that the qualities that distinguish this rarefied group can be learned, practiced, and mastered. What's essential is the willingness to recognize and consciously break old patterns and establish new ones.

What's become especially clear to me over the years is how often, without even being aware of the fact, people stop themselves. The 15 percent never do. Indeed, where others see problems, as often as not the 15 percent see opportunity.

This recently hit me with renewed force on a transatlantic flight. A lifelong sports nut, I'd taken this rare opportunity to chill out and watch an episode of *30 for 30*, the ESPN documentary series. The episode in question was on the 2002 Duke lacrosse rape scandal, and it was at once riveting and infuriating. As those who followed the case will recall, it featured a corrupt prosecutor ready to go to any lengths to convict three Duke lacrosse players falsely accused of raping a young African American woman, abetted by a national press cheering him on. The unlikely hero of the piece appeared about two-thirds of the way in: a mild-mannered and unassuming attorney named Brad Bannon, the junior member of the team representing one of the defendants. The prosecutor, Michael Nifong, claimed to have rock-solid DNA evidence that would nail down what was already widely seen as a slam dunk, and the defense had only a few days to prepare for Nifong's expert witness. Into the breach rushed Bannon. Though he'd never so much as taken a math course in college, he buried himself in the office conference room with thousands of pages of raw data and a book called *Forensic DNA Typing*, staying there for three days and two nights; until, having mastered this impossibly arcane subject, he determined that Nifong had been hiding evidence that was clearly exculpatory. Which is why, soon after, it fell to the inexperienced and still unsure young lawyer to cross-examine the prosecution's veteran DNA expert on the stand. "You could see Brad's legs were shaking," recalled his client. "He was really scared."

"Listen," the firm's senior partner told him, "there's a difference between lawyers and great lawyers, and that difference is moments like this. You are a great lawyer, Brad. I've always told you that, but you've never believed it. You can do this. You will do this. And you'll do great."

Over the next two hours, Bannon proceeded to tear Nifong's key witness to shreds, along with his bogus case.

Sitting on the plane, watching the guy coming so fully into his own, I wish I'd been able to say it to him personally: "Way to go, young man—and welcome to the 15 percent!"

CHAPTER ONE

Fear Strikes Out

Rule one of success:
Don't be stopped by fear or failure

If there is a single dominant trait common to the 15 percent, it is what I will call a low fear factor. No matter the business or life endeavor, no one rises above the pack without being ready, when it counts, to completely put themselves on the line.

In a sense, this is so self-evident, it hardly bears saying. It's not for nothing "High risk, high reward" long ago graduated from truism to cliché.

Why, then, do so relatively few consistently act on that understanding? Why, for millions, is caution the first and final instinct?

I've seen it throughout my career, in all kinds of situations; seen it not only among those on fixed salaries—so understandably being protective of limited assets—but almost equally among those who seemed ideally positioned to take the leap. I know at least a dozen real estate investors, operating in locales as varied as New York City and the Pacific Northwest, who've done nicely for themselves during the go-go climate of recent years; yet, of these, a majority are kicking themselves for not having invested a lot more, faster, and built not just a few buildings, but whole complexes—since looking back, it seems such an *obvious* thing to have done. Why, then, did they fail to seize the moment?

In his book *The Undoing Project*, journalist Michael Lewis talks of something called "the endowment effect," which basically means we tend to overvalue what we already have in hand. Does this basic human instinct cause some to be unduly cautious when faced with the prospect of gambling and losing what they already have? They may not hit it big, and they are definitely settling for less, but at least they're sure not to crap out.

Start with this: the size of an individual's fear factor has nothing to do with brains, educational level, or age. Some time ago, I happened to catch a really sharp twelve-year-old on *Who Wants to Be a Millionaire?*'s Whiz Kid Week. He'd reached the $50,000-dollar plateau—meaning that money was guaranteed—and followed that by acing the $100,000 question. The next step was the quarter-million-dollar question, which was: "The Pilgrims lived in the city of Leyden before sailing to America. In which country is that?" Of the four possibilities offered, he immediately narrowed it down to two—the Netherlands and Germany. Earlier, the kid had been the very picture of breezy confidence, but now, faced with putting at risk half the hundred thousand he'd already won for a one-in-two shot at winning an additional $200,000, he faltered, and he finally decided to take his fifty grand and walk.

Incidentally—or actually not—when the host now asked him which he'd have chosen, he said, "The Netherlands," the correct answer. Rather than risk the loss of fifty thousand, he left five times that much on the table. It was at worst a 50–50 shot at the right answer with a payoff of 5 to 1. Any professional gambler would like those numbers.

Well, okay, understood, he's a kid. But the impulse—to fear taking the leap, even when logical—that's universal. Early on in my entrepreneurial career, in the early 1980s, I saw a classic case up close and personal, when I became partners with a pair of guys who'd started a small business that had terrific growth potential, as turned out to be the case. Both guys were smart, capable, and energetic, but when I was working with them it soon became clear that they lived on opposite ends of the fear factor continuum. One was the driving force in their partnership; the other, while extremely competent, was rather uneasy about the risk. Where the first was as aggressively entrepreneurial as anyone I've ever known, always seeing possibilities, not limitations, his partner could be obsessively focused on the multiple ways things could go wrong. When they sold the company, the first guy immediately used his share of the proceeds to start another, which would also prove successful, and since selling it to Sheldon Adelson, he has continued to move from success to success; indeed, I invested in another new venture of his just recently. The other guy? Though he'd talked of moving to Hawaii to run a second business they had in mind, he suddenly decided—not joking here—that he was afraid to fly, so instead, took his four million from the sale and retired, got a nice house on the water with his wife and kids, cut down his overhead, and has lived quietly on those funds. In his mind, he won the lottery and cashed in.

Nothing wrong with that. He was a good guy, and I hope he's happy. But did he stop short of realizing his full potential? Let's just say this: The 15 percent would take the life of guy number one, worries and all.

What makes for a low fear factor?

The answer is as complicated as human nature itself. But it begins, on a gut level, with a dual recognition: that, ultimately, we are on our own in this world; and, for that very reason, we are built to be strong, capable, and resourceful. There is no reason to fear risk or to cling to security, when it becomes a life creed, born of personal experience, that even the harshest setback need be no more than a temporary inconvenience.

But perhaps asking what makes for a low fear factor is asking the wrong question. Perhaps the better approach is asking what causes fear.

Jeff Stibel, an entrepreneur and brain scientist, has surmised that the human brain simply has a bias toward negativity. "Bad things loom larger in our minds than good things. We evolved that way because paying attention to dangers is necessary for survival." Brain science actually created a name for this quirk within our brains. It is called "availability bias." "When we see negative news, we do not put it in context . . ." Stibel notes, ". . . a report of a murder in the town next door makes us think killings are common, even though we only have one example."

Additionally, Michael Lewis points to the work of two psychologists, Daniel Kahneman and Amos Tversky, who determined that most people get greater pleasure in avoiding loss than in experiencing gain. Put another way, the happiness of receiving gain is smaller than the unhappiness of loss. Basically, people make decisions to minimize regret.

In that sense, I was lucky. Having had what most people would consider a tough childhood, I had little to lose. "We were poor, but we didn't know we were poor," goes the classic line of many who achieve great success. That wasn't me. I *always* knew how poor I was, and I hated it.

There is much to be said for starting from a place where you have nothing. With nothing to lose, the great fear is not so much failing as staying where you are; and you also realize that there's no one who will change your life except for the guy in the mirror.

Me, I figured that out very fast. In fact, I vividly remember the day, even the moment, when it hit me with full force that, no matter what, I had within me the resources to surmount my circumstances and survive.

I was in third grade in Cuba, Missouri, at the foot of the Ozarks. It's a resort area now, but this was the mid-1950s. It was a time when for fun, kids hung out at the dump shooting rats with .22s. Cuba was a town of less than a thousand people—one schoolhouse, grades three through twelve, one classroom for each grade—and I was in class that afternoon when a tornado warning came. We got those fairly frequently, but this was supposed to be a bad one, and they were clearing everyone out, calling parents who came rushing over to pick up their kids, as other kids zoomed off on their bikes. I didn't have a bike—I walked the three miles to school from our rented place outside the city limits—and my mom was stranded at the house with my baby sister, and she didn't have the car, anyway. My dad did, and, as usual, they couldn't track him down. So after half an hour, the only ones left were me and the couple of teachers still trying to get hold of my dad.

But, again, this was a different era, nothing touchy-feely about it, so I wasn't surprised when one of the teachers said she was sorry, they couldn't wait any longer, and neither offered me a ride home. They were rightfully concerned about their own families. Protecting the kids had a different definition in those times; after all, they were telling us we'd survive a nuclear attack by hiding under our desks.

So, I start walking home. Only about a mile of it was paved, then it was dirt roads and paths through pastures and dense woods.

At first it was okay. The walk itself was nothing new, I'd made it a hundred times before. But as I got off the paved road to the dirt one, suddenly it got totally dark, like there was a solar eclipse. We kids had grown up terrified of tornadoes to start with—you'd hear all these stories where they picked you up and dashed you to smithereens against a tree or a building—so immediately I know I'm in trouble. It's pitch black and totally still, and all the normal sounds of birds and insects are gone, because the tornado's just sucked all the life from the environment.

And all at once it hits me with full force how totally alone I am, and I get as scared as I've ever been in my life. No houses anywhere, no grown-ups. All I want is to be home with my mom and baby sister. Maybe I should turn back, I think, then instead, I start frantically searching in the dark for someplace to hide, a hollow in a tree or a ditch to jump into, *anything*.

But, just as suddenly, that passes and I'm absolutely calm. So calm, I'm sure it was even measurable biologically, that my heart rate slowed and blood pressure went back to normal. And I think: "If I'm going to get home, there's nobody's who's gonna get me there—but me."

I know it's funny to say of an eight-year-old boy, but it truly was a "man up and go forward" moment.

There's an expression I've used a lot over the years in business—"Sometimes, you just have to lean forward and hope your feet keep up with you before your face hits the ground." This was the first time in my life I'd felt that at the very core of my being. *I've just got to keep my feet moving down this path, and I've got to not be scared, and I'm going to get where I need to go.*

So that's what I did. I got home. As I approach the house, I can see my mom waiting for me at the open screen door, my baby sister, Deb, in her arms, wrapped in a blanket. Mom's ready to grab me and dive into the ditch in front of our house, because we don't have a storm cellar, and she wants to get us far enough away that we won't be hit by flying debris. At eight, I was now the man of the house, so I was now on tornado watch. For some reason, I remained calm. Overcoming my fear was empowering. The feeling was almost euphoric!

A couple of minutes later, the tornado passed, real close, but far enough away that we were hit only by the ferocious rain that followed.

I don't know if my mom even noticed or understood what I had gone through, but after that I definitely thought about myself differently. Every time I faced any serious life test going forward, I'd not just know, but often consciously think: "I'm on my own. This is my journey. I've got to handle this." I thought it every time I changed schools—twenty-one times in ten years. I thought it the first day I reported to basic training in the military, the first time I walked into a courtroom as a lawyer to try a case, and hundreds of times since as a businessman and entrepreneur. It's sort of a pep talk I give myself, because, in one way or another, the tornadoes never stop coming.

I later learned that what I so vividly experienced at eight years old is explained by Canadian psychiatrist J. T. MacCurdy, who analyzed the courage of ordinary people during the Nazi bombing of London. He found that rather than provoke the expected mass hysteria, for most the sight of death and destruction actually had the opposite effect. It left survivors feeling empowered, the "near miss" experience producing a sort of determined calm. Having overcome their fear, they found themselves more secure, confident, and decisive.

The "near miss" I experienced at eight years old had the same effect—and in my case, it was permanent.

I knew, or at least thought, I could survive anything life threw at me. "Risk" took on a whole new meaning. Far from paralyzing, it was energizing, serving to clear my mind and sharpen my senses—as it does for every member of the 15 percent. Knowing you're wholly on your own definitely accelerates the process. For the 15 percent, poverty and/or adversity victimized them. They hated it—but they lived. While generally these types of victimizations create lifelong victims, for the 15 percent it was just a near miss. It made them stronger. Better than that—it made them fearless. They would never see themselves as victims again.

Wondering where my dad was that long-ago day? By then, I already could have told my teachers they were wasting their time trying to track him down. If they found him at all, it would almost surely be in some bar.

He was a walking tornado himself, a constant threat to our little family's well-being. He'd had a tough war, steering Higgins landing craft in the South Pacific, and between landings these young men were pretty sure they would die in the next landing. As a result, my dad drank so much he'd have an alcohol issue for most of his life. I didn't know that then, I just knew I couldn't count on him, since he was AWOL from our family. For 90 percent of my childhood I was without a dad in my life. Though he was alive, for all practical purposes I never had a father.

My father also spent some time in jail. And, needless to say, the statistics associated with having a parent incarcerated are daunting. Psychiatrist Felix Brown discovered that prisoners are two to three times more likely to have been raised without one of their parents. Malcolm Gladwell calculates that "having a parent incarcerated increases a child's chances of juvenile delinquencies between 300 and 400 percent. It increases the risk of a serious psychiatric disorder by 250 percent."

But, too, he adds, "one time in ten, out of the despair rises an indomitable force."

For me, my father was just another disadvantage to be overcome.

A tough, imposing guy, six foot two, with bulging muscles, my dad was a brawler who'd still be getting into fistfights in his late fifties. He was in the awnings business and would hold one of these heavy metal awnings up with one hand and screw it into the wall with the other. A real guy's guy.

But I'd started to get his number the year before the tornado, when I was in second grade. We moved five times that school year, in three different states. We started off in Cuba, because he'd been trying to set up a business called Glow Light with his brother; to a little kid, that was exciting, and I just loved that name. But they had a major falling-out after my dad started going on three- and four-day binges, drinking up the profits, and they ended up not talking for years afterward. From Missouri, we moved to Phoenix, Arizona, which he figured would be a great place for awnings, then to California, then back to Arizona, and finally back to Missouri; in fact, right back in Cuba. I'll never forget how surprised my best friend, Johnny Askins, was to find me sitting in the same classroom where I'd started the year!

None of those moves was easy. Each meant not just a new school, but the new bullies that came with it. Whenever I got to a new school, I'd have to fight somebody. I could only hope the bully was an empty suit, like Skut Farkus in *A Christmas Story*, and not actually all that tough. But sometimes the bully was *really* tough. No matter, I had to fight him.

Being the new kid all the time was miserable in other ways. At one place they'd be teaching phonics, then a week later I'd be at another where they taught whole language. I got so screwed up that to this day . . . well, let's just say thank heaven for spell-check!

Through all this, I'm slowly starting to realize what's going on. More and more I can see that my dad is completely irresponsible, and as we head back and forth up Route 66, I realize that's what my parents are fighting about, and I'm starting to hate him. The fights are so bitter that one day I understand that this is it, she's going to leave him, and get us the hell out, and she and I will go to live with her mother in Arizona. But then, almost immediately, she becomes pregnant with Debra, my yet-to-be-born little sister, and we head back to Missouri.

Of course, things don't get any better, maybe even worse. My dad would disappear for months at a time, then suddenly reappear. At one point he got picked up for writing bad checks, which was when he spent time in jail. That at least put a scare in him, and he dried out for a while.

The low ebb, for me at least, was something that won't sound like much at all to anyone else. It was one of those times after he'd disappeared for a couple of months, then shown up again. I'd been invited to a Halloween party dance, which was thrilling, because there was a little girl I *really* liked, with whom I was going to get to dance or maybe even play spin the bottle. Man, I'd never been so excited. Only we just had the one car, and now that he was back, my dad was driving it.

What happened would have been entirely predictable to anyone but a nine-year-old, but I was dumb and in love enough to believe his promise that he'd show up to get me to the dance on time. So, since we lived out in the country and you could see the headlights from far off, there I sat for hours in my Davy Crockett costume, waiting for those lights to appear. When I finally accepted that he wasn't coming, and started crying, my mom tried to console me. But what could she say? She knew as well as I that he was in a bar somewhere and had completely forgotten his promise.

But I look back on even that experience as ultimately useful. Being without my dad became what UCLA psychologists Robert and Elizabeth Bjork term a "desirable difficulty," one that makes one stronger, more self-reliant, more self-sufficient.

After that, I made a decision that I was never going to miss a dance again, not if I could help it; and I was certainly not going to depend on anyone else to get me there. And I've pretty much held to that the rest of my life. Even today, if there's something exciting going on, some event or especially an intriguing new project, I immediately look for a way to get involved. It's why I've had such a variety of businesses and legal experiences. If I've just got this one lifetime, why not experience all that I can? As the Eagles said in "Life in the Fast Lane"—"*everything, all the time.*"

But then there was my mother. A beautiful young girl gifted with brains and ambition, in another time she'd have been and done anything she wanted. Instead she married at seventeen, had me at eighteen, and found herself trapped in a bad marriage. Yet, for her two children, she was a bottomless source of encouragement and security.

No, she didn't go out of the way to protect me from bullies or many other trials of boyhood—quite the opposite, in fact. Yet, like many kids raised by parents of that era, that's just something else I grew to be grateful for. There's a story about the young Ronald Reagan one day running home to escape his bullies, and his mom actually refusing to let him inside until he'd dealt with them, one way or the other. If that was tough love, it bred the toughness and proved the love. My mom's attitude was the same as my teachers': "Hey, you're a boy, deal with it!"

She always had bigger things to think about, starting with her family's survival. Often our sole support, with my father out of the picture even when there, she'd get work as a hostess at high-end restaurants, where they liked to put her out front, to dress up the place.

But desperate as things sometimes got, she never stopped looking forward. Taking my hand, she'd pretend she'd studied palm reading and find wondrous things, new twists on how successful I'd be doing whatever I chose to—and rich. Implausible as that prediction might have seemed objectively, especially after another lousy day at another new school, I'd completely buy in. How could I not? She was my mom; who could know better?

No matter what, she just wasn't going to be held back by the mental and emotional chains that held down most people. Who knows where that came from? Her own mom, my grandmother, was a bit of a mess when she was young. Let's put it this way: when my mom was fourteen, she was hitchhiking, and a man picked her up and tried to molest her. She went home and told my grandmother—who ended up *dating* the guy. In fact, when my mom left home at seventeen to marry my dad, she took her two much younger brothers with her. Basically, she'd been raising them since she was ten years old.

I should probably add that my grandmother lived to be ninety-four, and my mom ended up taking care of *her*, as well.

My mom may have been only one of Norman Vincent Peale's millions of disciples, but it's a good bet none took positive thinking more to heart or practiced it more effectively. Though I was the first in my family to go to college, there's no question my mom was the breakout star in our family.

She somehow managed to cast even our desperate wanderings as a positive. By ten or eleven, I was sick to death of all the moves and starting to tote a major chip on my shoulder.

Since baseball was my thing, and I was pretty good, I'd have just joined a team, and made a few buddies, when we'd leave and I'd have to start all over again. In almost every picture from back then, I look like I've just come back from getting my ass kicked.

So, yes, I was perhaps beginning to question my mom's conviction that I was destined for greatness.

But, to her, there was a purpose even to that. It was a test of my character, so I should wipe the scowl off my face. And of course, she was right. It was infinitely more effective, bully/ass kicking-wise, to come across as friendly and more reasonable; not to mention that it prepared me for a career in which the capacity to readily adjust to new people and circumstances, and alter my style on the fly, would be a major asset.

When I was in eighth grade, I was at another new school and had to give a book report. The book I chose was *The Encyclopedia of Baseball*—which I now realize was completely bizarre, since it wasn't even a real book, just the statistics of every player in the game's history. But—what did I know?—to me it was endlessly fascinating.

Oddly enough, that proved a pivotal point in my academic career. I'd never been more than an average student, making some B's and lots of C's, but this time the teacher, Mrs. Lang, awarded the report an A+; and afterward she took me aside and told me I had a real gift for public speaking. I should, she said, pursue speech and debate.

With that, everything started to turn. I knew for sure I was good at something, and that made all the difference. I was verbally dexterous. In a public setting I could be charming, funny, or even, if need be, intimidating. It was a talent I'd always be able to fall back on, and I knew—when needed—I could deliver.

While I'd never known exactly what I wanted to do with my life, I'd always loved the lawyers on TV—Perry Mason, Owen Marshall, *The Defenders*—and now what had been a vague notion became a certainty: I was going to be a criminal trial lawyer.

Thirty years later, I looked up Mrs. Lang, then in her eighties, and had her and her husband over for dinner. It was important to let her know the difference she'd made in my life.

Not that my newfound determination to try to become my generation's Clarence Darrow was yet evident in my *other* grades. I started tenth grade at Anaheim High School, where I regularly cut class, and even when I showed, it's not like I was *there* there. For the first quarter of tenth grade, I got an F in Spanish and three D's.

But that was the one great advantage in ever-changing schools in the precomputer era: constant fresh starts. Because after that quarter we moved across town, and I ended up at Magnolia High, one of the best public schools in the area. Within a few weeks I had my first real girlfriend, Gail Stilwell, and it was her hard-and-fast rule that we had to study before we could make out. It wasn't until the end of the semester, when my grades from my old school came in, that anyone had any idea what a screwup I'd been, and, by that time, my teachers all thought I was smart. My Spanish teacher was especially baffled, trying to figure out how I'd gone from an F to a straight-A student in just a few months.

By senior year, as captain of Magnolia's award-winning debate team, I was designated one of the top hundred high school speakers in the country, and though I was only around thirty-fifth in our class of three hundred, my fellow students voted me the honor of being the graduation speaker.

What few of them knew was that, technically, I shouldn't have even been a Magnolia student, since in the interim we'd had to move again, to another district. I was there only because I listed a friend's home address as my residence. I now realize that was an early example of my view that there were no problems without solutions. There was risk in not giving my actual address to the school, but it was a risk that would not hurt anyone but me—and it was worth taking.

There were a number of life lessons I picked up in those years, but one hit with particular force and stayed there. Her name was Michelle Garrett.

Michelle was two years older than I, the homecoming queen at Anaheim High School when I was a mere sophomore, and she was, at that time, the most beautiful human being I'd ever laid eyes on. On first sight, I was totally, hopelessly smitten. When she'd come striding down the hall, I'd just back up against the lockers, mouth open. Gorgeous face, long blonde hair, the whole package.

Problem is, at that point in my pathetic life, verbal as I'm proving to be, I can't even imagine talking to her.

Enter my mom. "You should ask Michelle Garrett to homecoming," she said.

"No, I could never do that." I mean, positive thinking is one thing, reaching for the moon and actually grabbing it is another.

Mom continued, "Everyone else is so intimidated, she probably doesn't have a date. She says 'no,' no big deal. But you never know."

In my entire life, including negotiations with some of the world's most canny businessmen, I've never yet met anyone with such remarkable powers of persuasion.

Somehow, I got hold of Michelle's phone number, and, after obsessively debating the matter in my head for days, I finally picked up the phone.

Her mom answered.

"Hi, is Michelle there?"

"Hold on."

I could hear her calling Michelle to the phone. And in those few seconds, my nerve deserted me.

"Hello," she said, and I immediately hung up.

Thank heaven this was before caller ID or star 69—miserable cowardly worm that I was, at least I was safe.

The worst part? My mom was right—though she was homecoming queen, it turned out, honest to God, rumor was Michelle *didn't* have a date, and the school arranged for one of the football stars to escort her.

Over the years, I've replayed in my mind what *could* have happened.

"Hi, Michelle, this is Terry Giles. You don't know me, but I want to take you to the homecoming dance."

Maybe she'd have laughed herself silly at the gall of this dumb, pathetic sophomore. Or maybe not. The tough part is never knowing, because I gave up without trying.

It was a mistake I vowed never to make again.

CHAPTER TWO

Life Begins at the End of Your Comfort Zone

Playing it safe is the fastest way to . . . the middle

I met Patti, who would become my first wife, on a blind date in college—blind, that is, to her. I'd seen her at a distance—a lovely blonde with a striking resemblance to, yes, Michelle Garrett—and I made sure to get paired with her. We dated through the end of my undergraduate years at Cal State Fullerton and married after I finished my active duty in the military and before enrolling at Pepperdine Law School. Both of us worked summers at Disneyland.

It was alongside Patti that I first experienced the financial possibilities inherent in a low fear factor. We used to make the rounds of the game shows that filmed in Los Angeles, hoping to get picked as contestants, and often we were, chosen by a producer who, before the day's taping, would scout those of us standing in line to get inside, looking for those who might work well on TV.

Did I mention that Patti was the character Alice in Wonderland at Disneyland and I was a Jungle Cruise Guide?

Game shows became our part-time jobs—together we were on *The Match Game* and *Let's Make a Deal*—twice. Before I met Patti, I was on *The Dating Game* twice—won once, lost once. She was on *The Price Is Right* and *Hollywood Squares*. The first time on *Let's Make a Deal*, we ended up winning a travel trailer and a thousand gallons of gas, which we traded in for the cash equivalent of 35 cents a gallon. Big money for us.

But our great game show triumph came on our second appearance on *Let's Make a Deal*. Then, as now, it was a show that featured a real element of psychological/emotional complexity the others lacked. It might have looked to the casual viewer like great fun for the players in their goofy outfits, but for the contestants it could be a harrowing test of judgment and intestinal fortitude. For all the laughs, the essence of the show was the choices the contestant had to make on the fly, whether to stand pat with an okay prize or risk losing it by holding out for something better; in brief, a classic measure of "fear factor" combined with the "endowment effect."

We'd watched the show quite a lot, so we came prepared with a strategy—actually, several strategies, to account for each of the show's most common scenarios.

We arrive in our Disneyland costumes—me as a Jungle Cruise Guide and, more to the point, Patti as Alice, her blonde hair to her waist. We get selected by the producers to be on the show and, sure enough, right off the bat, Monty Hall, the emcee, gives us a key.

Based on our analysis, when someone was offered a key, nearly 60 percent of the time it would end up fitting something pretty valuable—a Jet Ski, a car, or a boat. Sure, occasionally it would be a lawn mower or a broken-down putt-putt, but the odds on a key were pretty good.

Monty says, "Do you want the key or take what's behind door No. 1?"

"We'll keep the key."

They open the door, and the audience moans—it's a Pontiac.

Monty expresses sympathy, he also wishes we'd taken the door. But, okay, now how about a deal? Door No. 2 for the key, no questions asked.

"No, Monty, we think we'll keep the key."

So they open the second door. It's a pint-sized donkey, and the audience laughs and cheers.

"Okay, do you *still* want to keep the key?"

"Yes, we'll keep it."

"Maybe I can make it worth your while to change your mind," he says, and starts slowly counting out hundred-dollar bills. "One. Two. Three, Four. Five. Six. Seven. Eight. Nine. Ten." A whole summer's pay in 1970 at Disneyland.

We exchange a quick look, and I can tell Patti's getting pretty anxious. "No," I say, "the key."

"Awwwlllright," he allows, certain we'll regret it, "Let's open the last door to see what your key fits."

The door opens and it's another car, a Chevy hatchback.

Of course, it could have ended badly—we might have driven home with a goat. If so, we'd have lived with it. But we started with nothing, and, given the variables, it was a risk worth taking.

As it happens, not long after that a Berkeley professor of biostatistics came up with a probability theory he dubbed the Monty Hall Problem, which purported to answer definitively the eternal question of which door to pick in which situation. It supposedly proved mathematically what we'd sensed instinctively.

Which is to say, my promotion of a low fear factor should never be taken as an endorsement of recklessness—quite the opposite. The idea is to be on the cutting edge, not the bleeding edge, to have the emotional wherewithal not to shy away from *smart* risk. We've all known people convinced the odds somehow don't apply to them, and who get high on their crazy bets. There's a name for those people—broke. Indeed, in business it is precisely such people who are the easiest prey for those with a keener sense of likely outcomes.

But while they may not flame out, the millions of ordinary souls burdened with excessively high fear factors also lose out in the long run. There aren't many products easier to sell than fear of loss. Not only is it the entire basis of the insurance industry, but a huge factor in many others. When I was in the car business we did phenomenally well selling extended warranties; and in the copier business, warranties were so profitable, we could actually sell the machines themselves at cost.

IBM's salespeople had a line they'd use in trying to sell their products to IT heads of other corporations: "You'll never get fired picking IBM." Forget the computer, they were pushing *job security.* It's the same reason large companies use major law and accounting firms—use the boutique guys and if things go wrong, you're dead meat.

Knowing all this, in theory, behaving otherwise—i.e., when warranted, *not* playing it safe—should be simple. So, for me, by the time I was graduating from law school, taking the risk of starting my own practice should have been a gimme.

Right, like diving off a fifty-foot board because Greg Louganis assures you it's okay.

So, absolutely, I'd never say any of this is simple. Or easy. In my case, I'd been telling people for years that my dream was running my own firm. But now that the moment was almost at hand, suddenly things weren't so simple.

Fortunately, by then I'd had an experience—and experienced an individual—that made it a whole lot easier.

It is February 6, 1969, and Patti's just turned twenty-one and I've taken her to Las Vegas to celebrate by seeing her favorite performer, Elvis, in a huge show at the International Hotel.

Just one problem. It's the hottest act on the planet, and tickets can't be had at any price. Well, okay, another problem—we're so poor that, never mind the tickets, we can't afford a motel room. Having arrived by bus, we're actually planning to stay awake throughout our entire twenty-four-hour visit, then catch the 2:00 a.m. bus home the next night.

To conserve our ten-dollar gambling budget, we walk the mile from the bus station to the Strip and walk into the Dunes Hotel and Casino, drawn by an "all-you-can-eat breakfast—99 cents" sign. Inside a crowd is going bonkers around a craps table, just like in the movies, because some guy's having a crazy run. He's maybe thirty years old, but obviously a highflier. And now—again, like the movies—he spots Patti and asks her to throw the dice for him. And, naturally she keeps rolling winners, as everyone goes crazy and crazier.

When she finally craps out, the guy cashes in his forty one-hundred-dollar chips and invites us to breakfast. Over eggs and everything else we can grab from the buffet without being too obvious, we tell him a little about ourselves, my law plans, her getting her teaching certificate, and he does the same. He tells us his name, Ray Wilson, and he's invented some kind of workout machine, which has led to his starting a number of workout facilities.

As we're walking out, thanking him for the food, he suddenly stops—then takes out the wad of hundred dollar bills he's won and sticks it in my jacket pocket. "Here," he says, "I'm taking a nap. Will you hold on to this for me until later?" and he starts walking away.

Stunned, I call after him. "Wait, hold on! How do I return it to you?"

He stops, turns. "Oh, okay. I'm at Caesars."

We retreat to a corner, and I carefully count the bills. There are forty of them—four thousand dollars! What a responsibility! Here we are at 6:00 a.m. in a strange city, with more money than I've ever seen in my whole life, and certain we'll be robbed any minute.

Not taking any chances, we find a bank and hang out for two hours in the parking lot until it opens, then have the cash converted to a four-thousand-dollar cashier's check in his name.

Having now wasted four or five hours screwing around, we rush over to the International to see if we can score tickets for the Elvis show. Fat chance. The guy all but laughs in our face—and, since I'm still only twenty, with my fake I.D. burning a hole in my pocket, we hit the quarter blackjack tables, thinking maybe we can parlay our ten dollars into a couple of thousand. This consumes maybe an hour.

Meanwhile, I've got that four-thousand-dollar check burning an even bigger hole in my pocket, and I can't wait to get rid of it. Figuring he must be up from his nap, we find our way to Caesar's Palace.

Sure enough, he's staying in an unbelievable suite on the top floor with his brother. Both of them are hanging out, relaxing in terrycloth robes.

When I hand him the $4,000 check, he looks momentarily confused. "Wow," he says, "I forgot all about this," and tosses it on a glass coffee table, where it slides across, and falls to the floor.

I wait for someone to pick it up, but it sits there, untouched. As vividly as I remember anything in my life, at that instant I think how incredible it must be to be able to be just thirty years old and toss $4,000 on the floor, and not even bother to pick it up.

"Listen," he says, "I really appreciate you guys doing this. Is there anything I can do for you?"

I tell him that's not necessary, but he insists. Finally, I tell him about our busted Elvis plans.

Five hours later, after an unbelievable dinner at the Riviera, his limo pulls up to the International with the two of us and him and his date. The show's about to start, everybody's already seated, but he walks over to the maître d' and hands him a wad of cash. I have no idea how much, but I hear the maître d' say: "Certainly, I'll take care of them." Ray asks for my contact information and leaves. A moment later the maître d' is leading Patti and me to our table. It's a steeped room, and we go down, and down, and down, until we're seated three feet from Elvis's microphone. It's so close our elbows are literally resting on the stage, and I realize they've had to move people back at the last minute to make room for the two of us.

Elvis was incredible, but how it all happened had to be the highlight!

Talk about from the penthouse to the outhouse . . . by the time the show ends, it's close to 1:00 a.m., and with no money left for a taxi, we have to sprint all the way to the bus station to make our 2:00 a.m. ride.

But this incredible guy has made a serious impression, and a year later, when Patti and I decide to tie the knot, we of course invite him to the wedding. His gift? Instead of a punch bowl or a set of cutlery, he has us contact his travel agent, instructing us to tell them we'll be honeymooning for two weeks in

Hawaii, staying at the brand-new Hilton Rainbow Tower on Oahu, the Rock Resort Mauna Kea on the Big Island, first-class airfare both ways—and to forward the bill to him.

Amazingly, in 1971 the bill came to almost exactly four thousand dollars.

By then I'd figured out he assumed we'd keep that wad of cash when he handed it to me in the Dunes, which is what some people might have done. But if that had been karma, it definitely would have been the wrong kind and have left a far less valuable lesson.

As it was, he served as an example that has stayed with me ever since. The first bona fide member of the 15 percent I ever knew up close and personal, he was entirely self-made, having through incredibly hard work parlayed a single small exercise facility into a miniempire of several dozen. More, far more, he'd done it while remaining the very embodiment of generosity and grace. Through him, I saw not just a world I suppose I'd known existed but seemed impossibly inaccessible—flying first class, riding in limos, staying in great hotel suites—but how, done right, achieving the fantasy comfortably coexists with character.

Cut to three years later. I'd been working part-time for two of the top criminal lawyers in Orange County, each with his own firm, which they wanted me to join when I completed law school and passed the bar. Both were great guys for whom I had maximum respect.

One of them pushed pretty hard. His opening pitch was very seductive, and he kept sweetening the deal. It was 1974, and I'd have a starting salary of $40,000, which to a broke twenty-five-year-old sounded like all the money in the world, and all the autonomy I wanted, plus a car and a hundred dollars in cash a week in walking-around money to impress clients.

The other guy didn't push at all. "Look," he said, "I'd love to have you. But if you're ever going to go out on your own, this is the time to do it. What's your overhead now?"

"Around $350 a month."

"So, what do you have to lose?"

He was telling me what I already knew—that once I got locked into a salary and had a better car and house, it would be that much harder to take the risk and break away. I could already see other lawyers my age starting on that path, especially those in the big civil firms, working sixteen-hour days pushing to make partner. In fact, nowhere did the universal truth seem to be truer than in the upper echelons of the legal profession: Getting what they thought they wanted only left people miserable.

I remember a trip to Sedona, Arizona, where I was introduced to a guy who was a kind of death coach, preparing people to die. He had all kinds of stories, but the one that stayed with me was about a wonderful little old lady, close to one hundred years old, who confided she had only one regret: that she'd only had sex with one man—her husband—in her entire life. "But you know, that's typical," he told me. "I've never had anyone with nearly as many regrets about what they did in life as about what they didn't do."

"People make decisions to minimize regrets," as the cognitive psychologist Amos Tversky summed it up. Exactly, and at the end of life regret *that* decision most of all.

In December 1974, I sat down and talked to Patti, who told me what I needed to hear: Yes, going to work for Mike McDonald's firm was enticing, and it would be comfortable. *But being in the comfort zone had never been the point; discovering what lay beyond it was.* Not that I really needed reminding. The next day I let him know I'd decided to go off on my own.

CHAPTER THREE

Visualize the Future

**Figuring out where you want to go is the
first step to getting there**

When I began my law practice, it was with the goal of making $40,000 a year, what my salary would have been if I'd taken Mike's offer. I figured I'd be cheating myself if I made less.

In fact, that first year, 1975, I took home only $25,000.

But my second year, I took home $75,000.

The third, $125,000.

The fourth, $300,000.

And by the end of the fifth year, we had thirty-five lawyers in the firm and over a hundred employees total, and we were making six hundred criminal court appearances a month throughout California and neighboring states, making us one of the most successful criminal defense firms in the West. Over the first eight and a half years, I would personally try ninety criminal cases to verdict, including thirteen murder cases and three death-penalty cases.

How did it build so quickly? The truth is that I saw it before it happened. Great athletes will talk about the importance of visualization. I truly believe the first step in the building blocks of reality is what I call a "thought-tron." Before electrons and protons formulate into physical reality, all things first exist as an idea or a thought. The first step in creating any reality is seeing the future and aligning your consciousness with that vision!

Integral to that process is imaging one's best possible self in that situation. John Wooden, the brilliant basketball coach for UCLA in the 1940s, 1950s, 1960s, and 1970s, drilled into his players what he called his "Pyramid of Success." The top block of the pyramid was "being your best, when your best is needed." Physicality was not enough; mental toughness and preparedness were essential for success.

Here, in my case, is how the universe conspired to bring together opportunity, luck, and hard work to make my dream a reality.

My drive, my focus, every waking moment was on being a great trial lawyer. The cynic would say, "So what? That doesn't mean it will happen!" How wrong they are. Without having the term for it, I was also practicing *capitalization learning*—taking what I was already good at and getting better. I'd always been good in speech and debate, had logged thousands of hours in competition before becoming a trial lawyer. Now, in the real business of law, I was building on the strengths and gifts that had been God-given and honed over eleven years of practice in high school, college, and law school.

Going in, I may not have been the smartest guy around, but I started with an excellent piece of advice from a successful older lawyer. He told me that for the first hundred days after opening shop, I should give away ten cards a day to someone new. If I worked hard and did a great job for my clients, every one of them would become a salesperson, and I'd never have to worry about hustling business again. How lucky I was to be in the right place at the right time to get such sage advice. I could be the best trial lawyer on the planet, but without clients how would I, or anyone else, know it?

For the first few days, it was easy. There's lots of people in your life, they're happy for you as a newly minted lawyer, and *"Here, let me give you my card"* was a snap. But pretty soon ten cards a day is not so easy. I started stopping at different stores on my way home, pretending interest in furniture or antiques so I could give the salesman a card; and I'd get my hair cut every week, always going to a different barber; or wait for the fellow shopper who seemed a likely prospect before choosing my checkout line at the supermarket. This was my life, and I was going to do whatever it took to make it work.

There's a term for this, several in fact: persistent, relentless, aggressively single-minded. I was all of those to the nth degree, and I've never made any apologies for that. Ask anyone in the 15 percent. Such obsessive focus is as close to a prerequisite to membership as you can get. That said, as we know, being obsessive is not necessarily always the most endearing quality. It can lead, however inadvertently, to abused feelings and busted relationships, professional and otherwise.

What's equally vital is self-awareness. As no one gets anywhere close to the top without exploiting his unique blend of skill sets, staying there demands full awareness of one's weaknesses and making provision for those. It is important to understand how others perceive us, and why, and—when necessary—to alter our behavior accordingly.

That so many people are utterly unable to do so might seem incredible, if we didn't see it continually played out in

the lives of notable figures—especially politicians. From arrogance to hubris to contempt for perceived inferiors, some of
them, as Peggy Noonan writes, are simply "incapable of the
self-indictment and implicit growth that comes of taking a
serious personal inventory."

And so, too, are countless others, in every walk of life
and profession, destined to keep making the same self-defeat-
ing mistakes. Tell whatever story you want, but do not lie to
yourself. As disappointing as the truth about your shortfalls
may be, only by confronting that reality can you ever hope to
improve, or to at least protect yourself from those deficiencies.

My friend Werner Erhard may have said it best: "The
truth will set you free, but first it will piss you off."

I started my law career long before I met Werner, but I was
already taking that admonition to heart. My strengths were
clear to me from the outset, because I carried them with me
from childhood. I was adaptable, obviously. But I was also
curious about almost everyone and everything that crossed
my path.

Yet that was also a fair definition of a short attention
span. For while my focus was (and in fact remains) total and
intense while an issue is before me, I also get very easily bored
and quickly become just as intensely interested in something
else. I like the action. I enjoy putting out fires, so I have to be
careful not to start them, just so I'll have something to put
out. I hate that about myself. Even now it feels uncomfortable
to talk about it. But I cannot deny that it is true, and only
by recognizing that deficiency, and keeping it always on the
mental front burner, can I properly guard against it.

Knowing this about myself, I also knew that I'd have
to depend on others to focus on the details, dotting the i's
and crossing the t's; and, if things worked out, manage an
ever-growing staff. For, of course, in every business, it's those

who do the same things well over and over and over every day, grinding it out, who gain sustained success.

The secret to being a good manager, as the Yankees' Casey Stengel once observed, is "keeping the five guys who hate you away from the four who are undecided." Me? Given my fanatical work ethic and habitual bluntness in a business setting, I'd probably have alienated all nine the first day.

I always just accepted this as part of my nature. It was only decades later, in my midforties, as my first marriage was unraveling, that I stumbled upon the larger truth. I was seeing a marriage counselor, who, aware I was constantly starting new businesses and running in multiple directions simultaneously, asked if I'd ever been diagnosed with ADD, attention deficit disorder.

"Excuse me?"

At this, he begins asking about my childhood, so I tell him about all the times I had to move and change schools, and suddenly he interrupts with, "Tell me about that—what you're doing now."

"Now?"

Apparently, I'd been fiddling with the stuff on his desk, rearranging pencils and pens, getting them lined up just so.

"Just out of curiosity, what does *your* desk look like?"

Well, I tell him, I've always had a thing about neatness and order. "I always have my books and magazines over here, just so. And I have my pens here, blue, black, and red."

"Tell me more about your pens—does it bother you when there's not the same amount of space between them?"

"Well, sure, because I'm neat."

"You're not neat. You've got OCD as well, obsessive-compulsive disorder."

And the more we speak, the more I realize it was true. It isn't just neatness; I go crazy if my clothes aren't neatly hanging, color coordinated, or if one of my shoes is pointed in a slightly different direction from the rest.

But that led to a further realization. It was my extraordinary luck to have these two disorders working together in exactly the right combination. The ADD makes me bored easily, and want to do all kinds of different things, but my OCD forces me to keep it all properly organized. My OCD would have me stay home all day reorganizing my sock drawer, except my ADD makes me have to go out and buy companies.

Somehow, my twin weaknesses had merged into my greatest strength. Two disadvantages merged into another, *desirable difficulty*.

I didn't know all that when I started the firm, but from the outset it determined how I operated. For one thing, I swore that, no matter what it took, I'd return every phone call the same day. Even now, I've got to answer every email and return every call the same day. I don't have a choice, any more than I can stop myself from constantly updating my to-do lists; it's obsessively compulsive, it drives me crazy otherwise. I literally *cannot* go to sleep unless I get these calls returned.

Which turned out to be terrific for business, if not necessarily for me physically. I put my home phone number on my cards, which nobody else did at that time, at least no other criminal defense lawyers, and my clients—DUI defendants, drug dealers, burglars, murderers—weren't particularly careful about getting arrested during normal business hours.

Fine with me, I just wanted their one phone call to be the one on that card. Not only would my phone often be ringing half the night, but also, upon getting home in the evening, I'd usually have thirty of those little pink message slips in my pocket—people who'd called during the day and had to be answered. I soon discovered the best way to get through it all (or at least convince myself I was moving toward the light at the end of the tunnel) was to prioritize the calls from the hardest (where the guy was in unbelievable deep trouble or had serious personality issues) to the easiest (where they'd thank me just for caring about their case).

The grind was so relentless, it seems incredible to me now that I arranged my life that way. But in my late twenties, I hardly gave it a second thought. *Screw sleep, plenty of time to catch up on that when I'm old!*

What mattered is that it paid off!

"Listen," I'd begin yet another postmidnight call, "this is your lawyer, Terry Giles. I'm really sorry to bother you so late. I had a busy day in court, but I got a message you called, and I wanted to get back to you."

If I'd been representing big-time businessmen, they'd have been offended. But these were folks who didn't get a lot of respect from their lawyers, and they were just blown away.

Still, after a while it got to be too much. Some of them took serious advantage, rattling on about their problems unrelated to their case, while others just wanted reassurance another assault conviction wouldn't put them away for life. So, I changed tack. Instead of making myself available 24/7, I gave each client a pad of paper when leaving the office, with instructions to write down any questions or concerns for me to deal with on their next visit. That last part was key; it was understood on both ends that that next appointment was set in stone. Life was chaotic enough for these folks; I owed them that measure of certainty.

As our caseload grew, I streamlined the interview process, making sure to always get to the heart of the matter in fifteen minutes, tops. It was a talent I'd begun developing while working at the public defender's office the summer between my first and second years of law school. I still have

my little calendar book: I did 1,026 jail interviews that summer for the public defender's office. Young as I was, you do
some thousand-plus interviews over a two-and-a-half-month
period, and you're either really stupid or you get pretty good
at it.

As with the public defender clients, those I worked with
now were ethnically diverse and sometimes relatively unedu-
cated, but they could be quite sophisticated in street smarts.
Their survival IQs would be off the chart. The vital thing was
to establish within those first few minutes a relationship of
trust. The client would call me "Mr. Giles," and I'd say, "No,
no, please, I'm Terry." Then, as I tried to get a handle on the
alleged crime—whether they'd done it, how best to proceed
either way—I'd keep the legalese to a minimum.

I never played hide the ball with clients. If it looked like
bad news, I gave it to them straight and made it clear that I
expected them to come clean in return; if they held back, and
I got blindsided in court, they'd be the ones to pay the price.
That said, they could trust I'd give it my best shot.

None of that sounds like much, I know, but some of these
people had been through the criminal-justice system most of
their lives, and in dealing with lawyers they'd run into a lot of
"Let's be clear on who's the alpha dog here." My clients knew
I wasn't a slouch, and I'd fight like hell for them. My win-lose
record was exceptional. But they also knew I wasn't going to
beat them up in my office to prove it or try to get them to take
some deal because it made life easier for me. If there *was* a
good deal on the table, I'd try to explain why I thought so in
the most straightforward possible way. Most of the time, they
took it, but when they didn't, I didn't press it or make them
feel wrong. It would be: "Okay, if that's your choice, we'll go
to trial. As long as you understand that if we lose, the penalty
could be that much stiffer."

Clarity was key. It's amazing how often something we think we're saying clearly is heard by the listener to mean something very different. These were sometimes literally life-and-death situations, and I didn't want that to ever happen, and I have no reason to believe it ever did. Truthfully, my clients knew I cared about them. In return, they cared about me. I did a good job for them, and they loved to tell everyone how they had the best lawyer. The practice exploded upward.

Communication had always been one of my strengths, but it now became something even more. Indeed, I would come to regard it as one of the three C's—along with consciousness and conduct—that are the main highways on the road map to success, not just for me and the 15 percent, but anyone. If we *consciously* envision our goals, consistently *communicate* those intentions clearly and without equivocation, and *conduct* ourselves in a way that always reflects our determination to make our goals come to pass, the universe will respond.

But again, I was also practicing *capitalization learning*. Being verbally gifted, I was a good salesman. Now, I was selling myself to my clients and my clients to a judge or jury.

This was my outlook as I launched my firm. I knew where I had come from, had no doubt where I wanted to go, and was already figuring out the shortest route to get there.

My first case as a lawyer was—what else?—a DUI (Driving Under the Influence). There I am, a brand-new lawyer, and things are looking pretty good, because two cops have written reports on the case that contradict each other, and I'm ready to take them apart on the stand if we go to trial. So, I meet beforehand with the DA, who happens to be woman, in a pretrial setting. I point out the conflicting reports. She glances at the reports thirty seconds and bursts out with: "Fuck! These fucking cops can't even write a fucking report! Fuck 'em, I'll dismiss the case!"

Welcome to the criminal justice system.

No problem with the outcome. But at heart I was still a good country boy from Missouri. And, at least vulgarity-wise, this was still a pretty innocent time even in hip America. Not only had I hardly heard cussing growing up, I hadn't at college or law school, either.

But it doesn't take long to learn the ropes, linguistic and otherwise. In judge's chambers, or when I was dealing with the DA, pretty soon I was dishing out the same language as everyone else. Behind the scenes, both the language and attitudes were as much those of the people in the orange jumpsuits as those in the suits and ties. The courts were a high-speed sausage factory, everything loose and crazy, with justice only an occasional by-product.

I had my first murder case my first year. A conviction. Ruben Barella was his name. Bad facts. A total of twelve eyewitnesses. It was a drive-by shooting where Ruben, while driving his car, shot a kid in a car he was passing. The streets of the barrios in Santa Ana, California, were a war zone, and Ruben was the president of the area's largest Mexican gang. There were four people in the other car, three people in his car, and several people on the street, but he was the one who pulled the trigger. Turned out the victim had stabbed his brother. We managed to keep the jury out for three days, but he has now been in San Quentin for over four decades. The facts were impossible, but I still feel bad at how this young man's entire life was wasted by ten seconds' worth of bad decisions.

Of course, jury selection is everything, and it's a skill in which I took a lot of pride. I've always been good at reading people—it's something that's paid huge dividends over the years in business—and back then it won me more than a few eminently losable cases.

Half the battle was keeping off the lemons. Remember Newman, the work-challenged postman on *Seinfeld*? You can't imagine how many postal workers we had on our juries. It's because USPS employees are on full salary during jury duty, no matter how long, and, since they hate their jobs, it's a paid vacation. They're not there to listen to evidence, especially not complicated evidence, as much as they're there to relax. A big part of my job was to entertain, so as to get the jury's attention, then simplify the story line into basic human emotions. Right or wrong, that was how most people made decisions. Finding the equivalent of twelve people good-and-true was a direct product of me being the best communicator in the courtroom.

I did have two favorite kinds of juror. First were older, heavyset black women. Why? Because they were empathetic and caring, some of the sweetest and kindest people I ever met, and there was a chance they had sons or relatives who were or had been in custody. All I had to do was remind them that this defendant was somebody's son, and I at least had empathy going for my client. Second—and this went against conventional wisdom—were police officers' wives. And if they were ex-wives, that was even better. I should say right here that I have great respect and admiration for police officers; they have an impossible job, and thank goodness they're there, dedicating their lives to the protection and well-being of the rest of us. As a defense attorney, I'd sometimes have to be rough with cops on the stand, but I'd always go up to them afterward and let them know it was just business.

Part of that is understanding cops *can't* always be honest or adhere strictly to every rule. They're out there, their lives on the line, having to trust their gut; but afterward, writing up their reports, they must justify every stop-and-search and arrest. So, if a cop claims he searched the glove box because he smelled marijuana, and happened to find the gun there, I'd never blame the guy, much as I and everyone else knew it was fiction. Because I also knew he knew the neighborhood, and probably also the guy he arrested, so he knew damn well there'd turn out to be a gun in that glove box.

Still, I can't tell you how many times the most influential juror in the jury room voting for not guilty was a cop's wife. The secret? They've spent a lot of time around police officers and have heard a million stories—good and bad. Besides which, since cops work terrible hours doing dangerous work, they are often stressed out and exhausted when they get home, making those marriages even more challenging. So, the wives not only know cops, they know them better than anyone. I'd always expect the DAs to challenge them, but they rarely did.

I considered my jurors to be potential salespeople. They had seen me in action, and I hoped they would spread the word. If at least half the jury did not ask for my card at the end of a trial, I was disappointed.

Armed with a strong vision of the future and practicing *capitalization learning*, I was confidant I could create and aggressively reach for the life I dreamed of. I was now in full gallop.

CHAPTER FOUR

The Underdog Strategy

Thinking outside the box makes dreams reality

Robert Schuller, the architect of the Crystal Cathedral and *Hour of Power*, once said, "You can get anywhere from nowhere." It may sound like a kind of riddle, but the underlying meaning is profound: when you have nothing, you have nothing to lose.

As the underdog, you have everything to gain.

Having grown up poor and moved twenty-one times by the tenth grade, I was always the underdog. And though I was now running my own law practice and making strides toward being the best criminal defense trial lawyer possible, I continued to embrace the role of underdog. Such a mind-set was more than merely a hedge against complacency; it was a key weapon in my psychological arsenal. Going head-to-head against prosecutors backed by the awesome power of the state—and often arguing on behalf of the weak and those regarded as life's losers—meant having to constantly outhustle and, yes, out*think* the other side.

Still, as Malcolm Gladwell has observed, "underdog strategies are hard." To win, the underdog must by definition be willing to "try things no one else dared or thought to do."

Which is also a pretty good way of describing what it takes to not just make it to the 15 percent—but stay there.

My two breakout cases came a couple years into my practice. Though they differed dramatically in their particulars, both involved gruesome deaths and garnered a lot of press. Indeed, what they had most in common was precisely what made them so useful in setting me apart from my competition: on the face of it, both looked all but unwinnable. I knew going in that the only shot to prevail would be to do the unexpected, pulling a rabbit out of the metaphorical hat—and doing it with as much drama as possible.

Set in California's rural Mono County, I think of the first case as "Mono Madness."

Only the killer knew which one died first.

All that was known for sure is that their hands were tied and the last thing that went through each of their minds was a .22 caliber bullet, fired at point-blank range through the back of their heads.

While the slugs were never found, the coroner surmised that both were killed with the same gun—a .22 rifle. If true, then one of them heard or even saw the other die—with the knowing expectations that it would be their turn in just moments.

I'm certain that the killer felt put out at having to kill Keith and Judy at that particular time of the year. It was freezing cold, and the ground was rock solid. Digging the makeshift graves was hard work, which explains why the holes were so shallow.

The next spring two hunters spotted a bear coming out of hibernation. Hungry and smelling rotting flesh close to the surface, the bear was just settling in for what promised to be a filling meal. Two shots from the hunters missed this magnificent scavenger, who galloped off half full. The part of his meal left uneaten was grisly but recognizable as human. The sheriff was summoned, and Mono County, California, a modest rural community whose greatest allure was the Mammoth Lakes Ski Resort, was thinking about murder— not a good thought ever but especially bad for a place that counts on tourism. There is nothing like the rumor of two travelers being murdered and buried in the woods to impact occupancy rates.

Paul Coatney was considered strange—even by the few people who knew him and didn't find him offensive. He lived in a trailer, always had his .22 rifle at close hand, and was often referred to as "the idiot of the county." This less-than-kind term referred more to his personality than his IQ. He had a voice quality that would remind one of fingernails on a chalkboard, and I am certain that his unreasonable arrogance came from layers of inferiority complexes as opposed to any success, at any time, on any level, during his mostly unhappy life. Paul was trouble already happening. A man who was determined to make others as miserable as he was. His parents were estranged, his wife was leaving him, and his life was devoid of any friendships or even meaningful relationships.

Keith and Judy had only been in town a couple of months and were renting a room. They had little by way of physical possessions, appeared to everyone to be inseparable, and had intentionally selected a bohemian lifestyle. The fact that they knew and conversed with Paul signaled how new they were to the community.

But early in the morning on the last day anyone saw Keith and Judy alive, Paul picked them up in his vehicle outside their rented room. The landlady, while retrieving her paper, saw the three of them leave in Paul's car. They seemed rushed, and she sensed stress with Keith and Judy. She later recalled her last thoughts that morning were why such a nice couple were hanging around Paul Coatney and why weren't they dressed warmer. What the landlady did not notice was that Keith and Judy were so rushed that morning that Judy forgot her purse. It would still be hanging on the footboard of their bed when the sheriff's deputies would finally search their room.

By all accounts, Paul took Keith and Judy that morning to the home of J.C. J.C. was a very good-looking and popular young man in Mono County. He was a natural athlete, and everyone knew him. He lived well, especially since he had no visible source of support. But no one thought much of it, because his father was successful by rural standards, and his mother had clout as the court-appointed clerk for the only superior court judge in Mono County.

Paul and J.C. both agreed that Paul had driven Keith and Judy to J.C.'s house that morning. Paul said Keith and Judy were nervous and had called him to give them a ride because of a problem with their car. Paul dropped them off in the driveway as J.C. was coming out of his house. Paul left without speaking. Paul knew J.C. didn't like him. That was the last time Paul says he saw Keith and Judy alive. J.C. agreed that Paul, Keith, and Judy stopped by his house, but he said he feigned being busy. He wasn't expecting them, and he wasn't interested in any quality time with Paul. He remembers the three of them leaving together. That was the last time J.C. says he saw Keith and Judy alive. The sheriff's office later would canvass the entire community. They would conclude that Paul and J.C. were the last two living persons to see Keith and Judy prebear.

Three weeks after last seeing Keith and Judy leave with Paul Coatney, the landlady reported them as missing. The sheriff's investigators searched their room. There was no evidence of foul play. But after finding Judy's purse, the investigators were sure Keith and Judy had not returned after they were seen leaving with Paul. They further surmised that something had happened to Keith and Judy. After all, if they had just taken off for parts unknown, Judy would have taken her purse. A formal missing persons investigation was opened, and Judy's purse was collected and stored as evidence.

For the sheriff and district attorney, the case was open and shut once the bodies were found. J.C. put Keith and Judy with Paul. A .22 rifle was the murder weapon and Paul's companion of choice. Additionally, though the bodies had spent months in the grave and were half-eaten by a bear, the coroner placed the time of death consistent with the general time Paul was seen picking up Keith and Judy. Besides, Paul was nearly unanimously disliked, and no one was surprised that he could be a killer.

The first trial was nearly a laugher. The case was tried in front of the one Mono County superior court judge. The DA put on his case with little rebuttal from Paul's court-appointed lawyer. J.C. testified, and his mother was very proud. Paul's estranged parents sat through the proceedings to support Paul. They were convinced their son was no murderer, yet there was no defense.

After closing arguments, the jury began deliberations. The first vote was thirty minutes into the discussion, and 11 voted guilty. The lone not guilty was a lady. Something wasn't right— it was just an intuition, but it was strong enough for *her to hold out for three days. The jury was deadlocked 11 to 1. The judge had no choice but to declare a mistrial and set a new trial date. Paul Coatney would remain in custody. His parents would decide to spend the money to hire a new lawyer.*

As I mentioned, my law practice was located in Orange County, California, and I was busy living my dream. At this point I was twenty-nine years old and had been a lawyer for four years.

When Paul Coatney's parents told me their son's story, I knew I would take the case long before the initial interview was complete.

An appropriate motion to change the venue of Paul's case resulted in us being assigned to Judge Terry Finney's court-room in South Lake Tahoe, El Dorado County, California.

I didn't know it at the time, but the trial would take six weeks and conclude in a hail of drama not even I could imag-ine. But all I knew in the beginning was that there was work to do.

First would be the investigation of J.C. It turns out his invisible means of support was possibly tied to drugs. Rumors were rampant in rural Mono County that J.C. was popular for more reason than his good looks. He was a supplier of drugs as they existed in that county at that time. We were told he would send his couriers to San Diego, wire them money, they would cross the border, buy drugs, smuggle them back across the border, and deliver them to J.C. in Bridgetown, Mono County. The good news was several people independently told us the same story. The bad news is none would testify. It seems J.C. had a side to him no one wanted to deal with. Oh, and there was one more piece of bad news: There was no evi-dence that Keith and Judy had anything to do with J.C.'s drug business. Without that connection, I was limited in my argu-ment as to why J.C. might have killed Keith and Judy. It was clear that one of my defenses for Paul was to accuse J.C., but without a motive and no one to testify that J.C. was a dealer, that route looked like a slope slipperier than "Dead Man's Run" at Mammoth Lake. But for reasons only explained by my unexplainable but absolute belief that this was the winning route did I proceed to trial with no doubt we could win.

Second, Paul's speaking habits and speech patterns were unbelievable. His parents had warned me, but hearing was believing. Paul testified in his first trial, and I could only imagine the smirk on the face of the DA at the prospect of him testifying again. But I needed Paul's testimony; he was the only one who could say that he dropped Keith and Judy at J.C.'s house on the day in question.

But an idea formed as soon as I read the transcript of Paul's previous testimony. What he said in the first trial was good and useful; it was how he said it that was cruel and unusual punishment to the human ear. I made Paul promise, on his life, that during the trial he would not talk in the courtroom—not even to me. I never wanted the jury to hear him speak.

The trial finally began, and two things were clear from the beginning. One, Judge Finney was a very good judge. His judicial temperament was excellent, his knowledge of the law was superb, and as a former trial lawyer in the DA's office in El Dorado County, he would let the lawyers in his courtroom try their cases. Two, the Mono County deputy district attorney and the chief investigator of the sheriff's office were pros. They were tough-minded and believed Paul was the culprit. They may have jumped to that conclusion far too quickly, but they were sincere in doing their job to the best of their ability.

During the DA's case in chief, he introduced a number of pieces of evidence, including Judy's purse, and called to the stand the landlady, the hunters, the coroner's investigator, and miscellaneous other witnesses about Keith, Judy, and Paul. This included an acquaintance of Paul's (he was even more goofy than my client), who said Paul confessed the crime to him. And, of course, they called J.C.

The alleged confession was ridiculous. The witness couldn't tell the same story twice, and a second-year law student could drive a truck through the holes in this guy's tale. But J.C.—now that was interesting. I knew enough about his illegal drug operation that I thought I could surprise him. Additionally, he wouldn't know I had no one available to testify about his business. My cross-examination was intended to exhibit a confidence that would cause him to lose his winning personality on the stand. As I asked questions about how his drug operation functioned, he panicked and lost his nerve. To my absolute delight, he started to take the "Fifth" in response to my questions—meaning he refused to answer my questions on the grounds that it may incriminate him. Everyone in the courtroom was stunned, and I was overjoyed. The DA immediately asked and received a recess, and J.C. disappeared into the hallway with the very stern faces of Mono County's legal elite surrounding him.

After thirty minutes, the court was called back in session, and the DA announced that J.C. would be given full immunity regarding his drug offenses. He would now be able to testify without fear of prosecution regarding his drugs. The decision was apparently made that a murder conviction outweighed any drug violations.

Back on the stand, J.C. admitted to drug dealing, to sending couriers to San Diego, to wiring them money, to having them buy drugs in Mexico and bring them back to him. But he steadfastly said he never had dealings with Keith and Judy and that they were not a part of his operation. I conjectured, in my questions, that Keith and Judy had burned J.C. for *money and drugs. As revenge, and to make a point, he killed this young, naive couple.*

But J.C. denied it vehemently, and I had no evidence to prove otherwise. Nevertheless, the jury was on the edge of their seats, and J.C.'s credibility was a wreck. I didn't need to prove innocence, just create reasonable doubt.

The DA now wanted to call Paul to the stand, an unusual request in a criminal trial because of the Fifth Amendment right against self-incrimination. But Paul had already testified in the first trial, and the DA argued this was a waiver of his right not to testify.

I, of course, argued that this particular right was so paramount to our system that a waiver had to be in the trial in question. Judge Finney knew, as well as the DA and myself, that there was no precedent at that time. Any ruling was dangerous and could lead to a reversal on appeal. It was now at the end of that week, and the judge asked us to do more research over the weekend so that the issue could be decided on Monday.

Monday morning, I laid out my plan in chambers. I reminded everyone of the difficulty we faced of a possible reversal no matter how the judge ruled. Then, I suggested we read Paul's testimony from the first trial to our current jury, in lieu of live testimony. I explained that the DA would get the exact testimony he so badly wanted, my client would voluntarily waive any rights in this case to allow the reading (which eliminates appealable issues), and the judge avoids a no-win situation.

The DA, only remembering the effects of Paul's testimony the first time, said he would do it. The judge was very pleased. I added one more condition. The reading would occur with the DA playing himself at council table and I would sit in the witness chair and play Paul. Because reading testimony is often done by the lawyers in a trial, everyone agreed, and we proceeded.

The reading took nearly two days, but, within the first two minutes, the DA realized he had been had. Paul's actual words were great and crucial for the defense, but now he wasn't saying them—I was. It was delicious.

By the time we got to closing arguments, I felt pretty good. We had avoided Paul's self-destructive speech habits, and J.C. had blown up his own credibility. There was, in my opinion, certainly ample reasonable doubt. But I still felt disappointed. From the outset, I had believed we would prove who the real killer was, and I would present it in dramatic fashion to the jury—but it hadn't materialized, and I wasn't used to that.

In closing argument, with great flair, I summarized the drama of the last six weeks, pointed out all of the reasonable doubt that oozed from this case, and made one last attempt to tie Keith and Judy to J.C. Because Judy's purse was in evidence, everything in the purse was also in evidence.

I had gone through it just like the DA and sheriff had. There was not much there except the usual things you would expect. But Keith and Judy were hippies, and the contents of the purse could be argued in several ways.

So, in front of the jury, I announced that someone can tell a lot about a girl by going through her purse, and I invited them, in the jury room, to examine the contents. I did my best as I poured out Judy's purse before them and began to argue the contents. An unpaid bill may reflect the need for money; a bent paper clip could be a "roach clip"; their bohemian lifestyle implied drug use. I may have made a few points, but I knew I never hooked Keith and Judy to J.C.

The jury was out three days. They were hung six to six when the foreman, out of boredom and as I had asked, began to go through Judy's purse. After fumbling around, he found something we had all missed—a false bottom. When he pulled the bottom out, he discovered a MoneyGram sent from J.C. to Keith and Judy in San Diego just two weeks before they disappeared.

Paul Coatney's incarceration was over. Paul and I were serious underdogs going into this fight. I pursued a strategy that was unexpected and dangerous, but we caught the opposition off guard. As a result, we won.

The second case—The Attic, for short—proved equally dramatic and demonstrated once again that one should be careful betting against the dog.

It was the hardest morning of their lives, which had now spanned over fifty years. She had been seeing someone else for some time. There were reasons—boredom, the drudgery of work and home, and, above all else, Marvin had stopped making her happy years ago.

The marriage of Marvin and Elizabeth Bains had been dying for a long time. But on this dreary winter day in early 1981, more than the marriage would die.

It started out like every other day with the two of them going to work, but something about Elizabeth's dress that morning disturbed Marvin. He followed her instead of proceeding to his job, and he caught her rendezvousing with her boyfriend in the parking lot of a grocery store.

Things dissolved rapidly. Yelling ensued, and the would-be suitor disappeared as Marvin and Elizabeth verbally squared off. The fight moved back to their home as their long- brewing ill feelings for one another bubbled to the surface. No one was going to work this day. I am sure that, as they pulled into their Buena Park, California, driveway, they had no idea that in forty-five minutes one of them would be dead.

It was Marvin who pulled out the shotgun as Elizabeth sat at the kitchen table.

One year later, at Marvin's trial, the coroner would describe the surreal scene as he walked into the room. Elizabeth was still sitting at the table, upright, as if she were about to have a cup of coffee. But the entire top of her head, from the bridge of her nose up, was gone. Well, gone wasn't quite right. Splattered all over the wall behind her was technically more accurate. Marvin was found alive, but he wasn't much better off than Elizabeth. His jaw and the entire left side of his face below his eye socket were missing.

Five empty shotgun casings were on the floor. Shots had blown apart the "cottage cheese" ceiling in the entryway immediately adjacent to the kitchen and pierced the roof above it. Standing in the house, investigators could see the dreary clouds that threatened rain through the two shotgun holes in the roof.

Marvin was in no position to tell anyone what happened. Among other things, his tongue no longer existed.

Because Marvin had threatened suicide before, the police theory went like this: Marvin discovered his wife having an affair, he confronted her in the parking lot, and the fight continued as they went home. Marvin pulled out the shotgun and fired two shots at his wife, blowing off the top of her head in the process. Staring at his wife still eerily sitting in the chair, Marvin turned the gun on himself. He braced the butt of the weapon on the floor and rested his chin on the barrel. Reaching down to pull the trigger, he inadvertently pulled his

chin off the barrel as he jerked downward on the trigger—
twice. Those shots shattered the ceiling and created the two
holes in the roof. Finally, on the third try, he got it right and
blew off a significant part of his face. Unfortunately, from the
investigators' standpoint, he didn't die. This meant he would
be charged with murder and, given his age, would die as a
resident of the California prison system.

It was a difficult case to defend. The trauma of the events
and Marvin's wound had wiped out his memory. He was the
only living witness to the events, and he couldn't remember
what happened and could no longer speak. Additionally, his
face was now grotesque. But any jury sympathy would be
countered by the pictures of Elizabeth sitting at the table.

Through an unbelievable odyssey of sign language, dic-
tion experts, and hypnosis, a defense theory was formed of
an accidental shooting and attempted suicide. If I was right,
Marvin would only be guilty of manslaughter and could be
out of custody in three years. By the time we got to trial, it
was a year after the event because of Marvin's hospitalization.

The defense theory was based on Marvin bringing out
the shotgun to threaten suicide. His wife, totally disgusted,
attempted to grab the weapon as he laid it on the table. He
tried to get it back from her and it accidently went off, killing her in the process. Now totally distraught, he tried to
commit suicide just as the prosecution suggested. Except in
my theory there was only one accidental shot in the direction of his wife, then he missed on his suicide attempt three
times and finally semisucceeded on his fourth try. My theory explained the five shots, but three misses and only two
holes in the roof was troubling. By the time I was hired,
nine months after the event, the home had been sold and the
ceiling and roof repaired. Pictures of the scene were all I had
to work with.

As I squared off against the district attorney, it came down to this—two shots at Mrs. Bains is murder. One shot was a possible accident and involuntary manslaughter.

During the trial, while I was cross-examining the chief investigator on a late Friday afternoon, he told me something I never knew and that was not in the police report. The home had been built in the early 1960s and, like many California homes, had no real attic or basement. However, there was a low, three-to-four-foot crawl space between the ceiling and the roof. Between the ceiling joints fiber insulation was packed in to help climate control.

I knew, from my childhood days in the Ozarks, that shotgun shells not only fired pellets, but a light plastic cup, which holds the pellets. If we could find those plastic pellet cups, we would know which shots were fired where. The police had only found one behind Elizabeth, although they admitted that all the brain, skull, and flesh debris prevented a further search for the other cup, which they felt no need to conduct. Also, one cup was found next to Marvin from the shot that impacted his face. Two holes in the roof supported the DA theory, but three missing cups kept my theory alive.

I questioned the investigator about the possibility of two shots going through the same hole in the roof—three shots and two holes. He thought it highly unlikely, and it had all been repaired. But what if the insulation in the crawl space trapped the cups as the pellets burrowed through, and that same insulation was still in the crawl space? Would three cups in the insulation convince him my theory was correct? Although the insulation had never been searched, and he thought it highly unlikely anything would be found after a year had passed, he agreed that three cups in the insulation would support my theory as opposed to theirs.

At that moment, in front of the jury, I had to make a decision. I could argue that if the police had done a search of the insulation at the time, they would have found the evidence I believed would have been there. That would be the safe route, but would it be enough to create reasonable doubt in the minds of the jury? Or . . . I could challenge the investigator to go into the crawl space with me and search for the plastic cups, but such a search could also help the prosecution.

Marvin and I were the underdogs, and the death and pictures of the scene were grisly. I calculated that if we were to win, we had to do the unexpected. With a sense of confidence, a feeling I had felt many times, in that split second in front of the jury, I challenged the investigator to search the crawl space with me the next day—Saturday. He had little choice but to agree. Court ended that day as I looked at the jury and announced, "The answer is in the attic."

As luck would have it, it was a very hot Saturday morning, and the attic was stifling. Both the investigator and I were beginning to drip sweat as we crawled around running our fingers through the insulation. After about ten minutes, I actually found one of the cups entangled in the insulation, which gave me great hope—but then I was reminded of why this search could be a disaster. What if we only find one or two cups? I will have inadvertently helped to prove the DA's case.

Then it happened. Running my hand down through the insulation, I felt a sharp pain and pulled my hand back up to see that I was bleeding. The investigator then carefully began to remove the insulation a little at a time so as to discover what had cut me. What we discovered was a cross timber that had been fractured upward with a direct hit from a shotgun. It had buckled and splintered but did not give and remained hidden in the insulation. The buckled beam and two holes in the roof was evidence of our three-shot theory.

On Monday the jury was released, and the DA dismissed the murder charge. Marvin pled guilty to involuntary manslaughter, and the Los Angeles Times *called it a "Perry Mason ending."*

Marvin did three years in custody, most of that in prison hospitals. Sadly, two years after his release, using a handgun, he successfully committed suicide.

———————

To be sure, pursuing an underdog strategy can be hard, even dangerous to one's career, as it was in both these cases. It means doing the unexpected, taking real risks, and working hard to make them pay off. But no one earns his way into the 15 percent without sometimes putting all the chips on the pass line and hoping to roll a 7.

When you are a criminal defense lawyer, winning big cases and garnering lots of positive press, interesting things begin to happen. For instance, I never knew what would be waiting for me in the office in the morning—a message slip might suddenly send my life careening in an entirely new direction.

The Hillside Strangler case was one of those.

The murders had transfixed—and terrified—LA, the pressure on the police growing ever more intense as more bodies of young women kept turning up on the hilly outskirts of the city. When the announcement at last came that they'd broken the Hillside Strangler case, it came with a startling twist: *two* men had been charged, cousins Angelo Buono and Ken Bianchi. Multiple murderers were highly unusual in a serial killing case. Still, Bianchi's confession to the Hillside murders, after he'd been brought in on another charge, was explicit, as in grisly detail he described how they'd used police badges to reassure their young victims.

Yet there was something about Ken's confessions that seemed forced and inconsistent. And when I walked in that morning and saw the message concerning Buono, who was incarcerated in LA jail, there was no question I'd take the case.

Quite frankly, Angelo Buono made my skin crawl. Though by now I'd met some pretty bad guys—Bill Bonin, for one, the Freeway Killer, who liked to punch out boys' eyes before he killed them—I never felt evil like I did sitting face-to-face with Buono. Beyond the complete nonchalance with which he talked about those poor dead girls, there was his appalling sense of entitlement. This perpetrator of these gruesome torture/murders was the biggest whiner you ever saw. I'd go see him about the case, and all he'd want to talk about was how they weren't giving him enough milk in jail, and how he needed me to go to court right away for an order to get him an extra carton. "Screw that, Angelo," I told him, "I'm not gonna bug the court about your milk. I don't give a darn about your milk; I'm trying to save your damn life."

Strangely, the evil I could handle, but his whining was too much! I did not think about it at the time, but now that I look back on it, I can see that the criminal law had begun to alter my perspective.

Nevertheless, I wasn't exactly displeased when we came to a parting of the ways over strategy. In the book *Helter Skelter*, about the prosecution of the Manson murders, Vincent Bugliosi talks about how, if Charlie Manson had pushed for a speedy trial, which was within his rights, the state, still trying to put together its case, would have been unprepared and at a major disadvantage. But, lucky for him, Manson's attorneys were looking to delay, as the defense usually does.

Well, I felt the same thing applied in Buono's case, since, beyond Bianchi's false confession, they didn't have much,

while on our end there was lots of reasonable doubt, starting with the highly questionable notion that the murders had
been committed by two men in concert. While we weren't
completely ready ourselves, I was confident we could, at
worst, get a hung jury.

But Buono's other lead attorney was strongly in favor of
delay, and Angelo had been talking to lots of jailhouse lawyers, who always subscribe to the theory that criminal cases
get worse for the prosecutor with age. Besides which, Buono
didn't like me any more than I did him.

Eventually, Bianchi recanted his confession, leading the
DA to seek dismissal of the case. All of a sudden, defense
delay looked like a pretty good idea. But then the California
attorney general stepped in, took over the case, tried Angelo,
and put him away for life. My strategy now didn't look so
bad.

According to Google, Angelo died in prison in 2002.

Thank you, Google.

Recently, codefendant Kenneth Bianchi, who is incarcerated in the state of Washington for the rest of his life,
contacted me and asked if I could represent him on appeal
regarding the Hillside Strangler murders. While I have always
believed Bianchi's confessions were forced and were untrue, I
could not represent him because of the obvious conflict.

Speaking of Vince Bugliosi, one day during the sixth
year of my practice, word got around the Orange County
Courthouse that he would be doing a hearing there that morning, so I gathered with the other young lawyers and watched
the legend perform. Afterward, everybody's filing out of the
courtroom, and Bugliosi walks past me, then stops and turns
around. "Are you Terry Giles?"

"Well, yes, Mr. Bugliosi, I am." I was surprised he even
knew my name.

"I understand you now have the largest criminal practice in California, is that true?"

"I have no idea—but if you say so, I'll believe it."

That was the entirety of the conversation. But I guess it was true. At that point I'd been in practice five and a half years and was long past having to hustle for business. On a Monday morning in Central Court we sometimes answered "ready" on forty or fifty cases and could have taken over all eight trial courtrooms in that courthouse. As a result, they would have to assign a special DA to negotiate our cases.

But that was the day I knew for sure that I'd made it as a criminal trial lawyer. Like every member of the 15 percent, before and after me, my dream was now my reality.

CHAPTER FIVE

Be Careful What You Wish For

Never be afraid to take stock and recalibrate

If anything so far suggests I might've been getting a bit full of myself, I'd argue I at least came by it honestly; I was good, had the record to prove it, and, if I ever forgot, there was usually something in the paper to remind me.

The *Orange County Register* was the region's major daily, and one year it featured stories on my cases 235 days. We made page one on thirty-five days that year, three times accompanied by my picture. It became almost routine to be recognized in the street or at the grocery store, and I pretty much forgot what it meant to have to wait for a table at crowded restaurants.

Think that might have been an ego boost?

Nothing wrong with that. Quite the contrary, in fact. No one's going to make it to the 15 percent, and stay there, without a firm belief in their own abilities and an unshakable sense that if played right, those abilities will take them where they want to go. Blowing one's own horn is fine, essential even, as long as it's part of a larger life plan—and kept in bounds.

But on the upward climb, sometimes that last part's not easy to keep in mind.

Starting with my legal career, I've learned the hard way that I get into the most trouble after a string of successes. Just when I start to think of myself as bulletproof, that's when I take one in the heart. Make no mistake about it—thinking you are bulletproof is ignorance, and ignorance is fueled by arrogance! I know, because I have been guilty of both.

Not that there wasn't a very real method to my courting of the press. Far from mere grandstanding, it was an invaluable weapon I wielded in defense of my clients. Prosecutors and cops in that era called press conferences all the time, putting out their version of the crime. Yet, back then, with the notable exceptions of guys like F. Lee Bailey and Melvin Belli, defense attorneys in big-time cases generally dismissed reporters with a curt "No comment." As a result, by the time the trial got underway, the world would already be convinced the client was guilty. Even if they got off, people would assume it was a miscarriage of justice and continue to make their lives hell.

I wanted to start educating the public from day one, and with that in mind, I'd call in the press any time I thought it might give us an edge. The one thing you could count on—I would look to do the unexpected.

And, hey, if the publicity also helped my business grow, nothing wrong with that.

Of course, it didn't exactly foster warm and fuzzy feelings among my colleagues in the criminal defense bar. An outsider by nature, I wasn't much for socializing to start with. Criminal defense lawyers being big drinkers, after court a bunch would always head down to the local watering hole, Reuben's, and I never joined in. That was never much of a problem until one day a reporter called and asked me why not. "Because I'm too busy interviewing new clients," I replied. It was a smart-ass comment, and I regretted it the moment it was out of my mouth, but the next day, there it was in the paper, and it certainly didn't help.

Then there was the great Christmas-morning caper.

I was sitting alone at home early that December 25th, sipping a cup of coffee, and since Patti and I had no kids, it's not very Christmassy. So, on impulse, I decide to head over to the Orange County jail and give each of my fifty or so clients in custody that Christmas five dollars to buy themselves Christmas candy bars on me. When I arrive, the place is pretty desolate, and, of course, I'm the only lawyer there. But the jailer on duty thinks it's a nice gesture, even if it was unexpected, and gets all my guys and brings them down to the holding cell. I see them one at a time, maybe two minutes with each. I tell them I'm sorry they're in custody and know this isn't a very merry Christmas, but let's hope that by next year they'll be back with their families, which I'm going to do everything in my power to make happen. And, by the way, I'm putting five dollars on the books in their name so they can buy themselves a Christmas candy bar. My clients seemed very appreciative, the whole thing takes me no more than a couple hours, and I don't think anything more about it.

Well, when I come back to work after New Year's, I must have two hundred messages from other inmates in Orange County jail, all wanting to fire their lawyers and hire me.

This went over so big with the Orange County bar they actually started an investigation, claiming I was paying money to my clients to solicit business for me behind bars. I had not followed up on any of those two hundred messages, so it was a ridiculous claim, and quickly dismissed, but frankly I didn't understand why, if it bothered them so much, they didn't do the same for their clients.

Doing those small things was so easy. For a time, we also bought Christmas gifts for all the court clerks and bailiffs, a fifth of liquor for the guys, a box of See's Candy for the women. Why? Because why not? These folks worked hard and were the backbone of the system.

Of course, the bar complained about that also, claiming I was bribing clerks and bailiffs. So that ended that. But of course, we then went around to the clerks and bailiffs explaining why they weren't getting their gifts anymore because the other lawyers had complained, so we still got all the credit without the financial outlay.

So, I was feeling pretty good about things—and, yes, maybe bulletproof. Everything was exactly like I had envisioned it. It was all perfect. Then I got the Fred Douglas case.

In the late 1970s, authorities were alarmed to find an influx of pornographic films coming into the United States from Mexico. Pornography was not, in and of itself, unusual. The first thing that set these films apart was that the girls who appeared were not freely participating.

The second is that the young women were often brutally raped and forced to do sexual acts during real torture.

The third: at the end they would be slaughtered on camera.

"Snuff" movies were a phenomenon sickening beyond all imagining. Yet there were actual buyers for these things in the United States. It was a shadow mini-industry. And now law enforcement was rallying aggressively to shut it down.

The Garden Grove, California, police department felt they had a "snuff suspect" in a man named Fred Douglas. Nine girls, prostitutes and female barflies from Garden Grove and

Santa Ana, had disappeared. Then a barmaid had come forward and told them that Fred had solicited her to help him line up, torture, and kill two women—and the whole process was to be filmed. She was terrified, and her story rocked this quiet Orange County city located right next to Disneyland. A sting operation was set up with two undercover female police officers posing as hookers. A wire on the barmaid would record everything Fred would say the morning he and the informant waited for the undercover officers to arrive. Sure enough, he bragged about what he was going to do to the girls. Every chilling word was recorded and later played to the jury.

Once the two female undercover officers arrived, the four of them headed for the San Bernardino desert, finally stopping in a remote canyon next to a small shack, at which point the police swooped in and made their arrest. Inside the shack they found torture devices and a meat hook, with what appeared to be dried blood, hung from the center of the ceiling. A massive search began for the bodies of the missing girls, but after much digging in the area, no bodies were found. However, search warrants for Douglas's home and shop turned up hundreds of photos. In the pictures the women were tied up and appeared to be in pain as various carpenter tools were being applied to their naked bodies. There were graphic sex acts being performed on the women by several unidentified men and Fred. Fred Douglas was held in custody and charged with the disappearance and possible death of the women.

It was Fred's son who called me. As a criminal lawyer, I thought that this hugely publicized criminal case just meant another round of "showtime."

My defense of Fred Douglas would turn out to be a classic, featuring the most dramatic cross-examination of my career.

Indeed, that the tapes and photographic evidence in this case could be overcome initially seemed impossible. But we set to work, launching a top-notch investigation of our own, and our investigators turned up evidence the police had missed in their search of Fred's premises.

The crux of the defense was that yes, absolutely, no question, Fred *was* a real sicko—but that didn't make him a murderer. What he was, in fact, was a classic bullshitter, and he made up all this disgusting crap to impress this pretty barmaid. The photos? They were faked, and the girls weren't really hurt but were alive and well.

Still, all that was window dressing. If we were to have any shot at all, I knew I'd have to destroy the credibility of their star witness, the barmaid. She was the one who'd nailed Fred in the first place, and who'd heard him recount his gruesome stories firsthand.

On the stand, the girl does really well on direct. She testifies in detail about his boasting of how he killed these girls, which makes the prosecution's playing of the incriminating tape all the more chilling.

On cross-examination, my approach is skepticism bordering on contempt. I dismiss her testimony out of hand as that of a woman scorned and looking to get even. "You were Fred's girlfriend, and he dumped you, isn't that right?" I demand. "You know very well it's not real, he just likes to talk dirty. You just made all this up because you're mad at him."

"Absolutely not!" she shot back.

"You *were* his girlfriend, weren't you?"

"No way!" she says, clearly offended by the question, which is easy to believe, since she isn't half-bad-looking and Fred is a gross, ugly slug of a guy.

"Well, you had sex with him, didn't you?"

"You kidding me? I'd rather have sex with animals than with Fred Douglas!"

"So, okay, maybe you weren't his girlfriend, but you two did a lot of necking, right?"

"Oh, God, my lips would *never* touch Fred Douglas!"

What no one knew, because in those days the defense didn't have to turn over evidence to the prosecution, is that the police hadn't found *all* the photos at Fred's place; there was a stash we found later, and it included twelve different angles of this witness performing oral sex on Fred.

So now I approach the bench to tell the judge I'm going to put these things in evidence, and the DA and the judge see the photos for the first time. The DA goes berserk, but there's nothing he can do; the barmaid is obviously lying.

Returning to my cross, I quietly lay the first picture in front of her. I don't have to say a word. Immediately—I mean *instantly*—she bursts into tears, just totally falls apart.

I resume my questioning. "Isn't that a picture of you? And isn't that a picture of Fred? And aren't you sucking on his penis?"

She's sobbing so hard, she can't even answer.

So, I just continue, laying down the photos and peppering her with questions, which she doesn't answer. And after each set of questions, I say, "Your Honor, may I pass this picture to the jury?" and the jurors are transfixed, studying these things.

I drag it out for thirty minutes, as their case just dissolves, because of course now no one can possibly believe a word she says about anything.

We win both the case and a lot of press.

Cut to one year later, I've now been practicing for eight and a half years. I'm on vacation in Maui, walking on the beach, when I'm tracked down and rush back to the hotel for an important call—no cell phones in those days.

Fred Douglas has been arrested for the murder of two more girls killed just six months after I earned him his acquittal. He ran to Mexico, and the law had been quietly searching for him. But now he's been arrested and extradited to the States. He wants me to represent him.

It was one of those moments on which life turns.

I don't have to think even a millisecond. "No," I say, "I will not be representing him."

He was eventually convicted and sent to death row at San Quentin.

But what remains most vivid in my memory are the moments immediately after the phone call. Back alone on the beach, numb, the thought ran over and over in my mind: *This is nuts! What am I doing? Why is the world a better place because I do what I do for a living?*

As a criminal defense attorney, I'd always viewed my responsibility as representing my clients to the best of my ability, using all the smarts, diligence, and guile at my disposal to achieve the desired result. And if, undeniably, sometimes that meant representing some repugnant clients, or pulling maneuvers in court that later gave me second and third thoughts, this is what the system calls for, and the results will show that I did it well.

But that is not to say it always went down right, or that the bad ones were easily forgotten. One case that left an especially tough impact on me was a drug-related murder, where my client was alleged to have thrown another kid from a plane. But since it could also have been accidental, or self-defense, I threw all sorts of doubt out there, most of which involved trashing the dead kid, and I got an acquittal, and that seemed the end of it. Except three or four years later, somebody tells me they ran into the dead boy's father, and he despises me so much, he says he'd kill me in a heartbeat if he thought he could get away with it.

I got a lot of death threats in those days, so another one wasn't in and of itself a big deal; but, maybe because the victim was so young, or because the father loved him so desperately, that one really hit me.

Yes, I was doing right by my clients; in that sense, no one could say I'd deviated from my commitment to fair and honest dealing. But was I doing right by the *world*? Or had I locked myself into the position of doing wrong—and then having to rationalize my way around it?

Fred Douglas wasn't the first, just the one that finally stopped me cold.

I was thirty-four years old, at the top of my game, with every confidence in my abilities, and a lifestyle I really loved. I had envisioned and produced exactly what I had asked for.

And now two innocent girls were dead.

As soon as I got back to California, I announced to my partners and associates that I was quitting the firm, and I never went back. I had arrogantly assumed that everything I did was appropriate. I had every right to be confident in my abilities.

But in reality, I was often doing good work—for bad people.

CHAPTER SIX

The Disney State
of Mind

Learn—and live—what has worked in the past

"Wisdom begins in wonder."

Though it was supposedly Socrates who said it, would anyone be surprised to find it credited to another visionary, Walt Disney?

One of the best things that ever happened to me in my formative years was getting to spend five summers during my college and law-school years working at Disneyland. I started just a few months after Walt's death, early enough that the Disney operation remained not so much a corporation as a mind-set. From day one, every employee was inculcated with core understandings and rules of behavior that, if taken to heart, greatly increased the odds of long-term personal and professional success. Indeed, I have used them to guide my team in every one of my companies I have started since.

Not, of course, when I first applied for the job, that it was "wisdom" on my mind. At eighteen, the operative word was "fun," and Disneyland, which seemed to employ half the college kids in Southern California, including legions of gorgeous girls, looked to offer more of it than any other summer job going.

At the employment office, I aimed for the top: the Jungle Cruise.

"Right," said the interviewer, who had to hire a lot more street sweepers and dishwashers than slick-talking guides, "everyone wants the Jungle Cruise."

Why not? Not only was it one of the coolest jobs at the park, it was the most lucrative; at a time when most summer jobs paid a buck twenty-five an hour, Jungle Cruise pilots got $3.50. This was because, for some reason, the ride operators at Disneyland were represented by the Teamsters, and I guess Jimmy Hoffa and the boys had negotiated the contract.

Skeptical as he was, the interviewer gave me the Jungle Cruise script and five minutes to study it—a snap, after years of debate prep. So, in the spring of 1967, I was cruising the mighty Amazon through Anaheim, perfecting my spiel and shooting blanks at passing hippos. All in all, it was a pretty cushy job: two ten-minute boat trips through the jungle, followed by two turns on the dock loading and unloading passengers, two more rounds on the boat, then a break. A twenty-minute break every hour!

After hours during the summer, various rides would throw parties. It was like being in a fraternity—and the Jungle Cruise was the top frat house, since it was a guided ride, we got to flirt with the great-looking tour guides and to wear neat uniforms, not those goofy outfits they had to wear in Fantasyland. Plus, since we all had to be quick and verbal, there were always some hilarious guys in the jungle. One guy had a variation on his standard talk he called his "vegetation spiel"—for the entire trip, he would ignore all the animals and just talk, with great earnestness, about the flora. He did it with a sense of humor that had the guests rolling in the aisles with laughter.

All the big rides in Adventureland and Frontierland would throw their version of a big party each summer—and the name of the party said it all. The Jungle Cruise threw the second most popular bash, called the "Banana Ball." But nothing topped the party the "Indians" down on the canoes sponsored. Everyone wanted a ticket to "Custer's Last Stand."

Yet as much fun as the job was, it was so much more. Indeed, it is the opposite of coincidence that so many of the people I got to know there ended up so successful in business, some as top executives with Disney when they opened in Florida. Quite simply, the Disney culture promoted in its young employees a degree of competence and personal accountability highly unusual at the time and, alas, almost unprecedented today. It also offered graduate-level instruction on the power of words.

The process began the first day on the job. We were instructed to use a specific vocabulary. Visitors to the park weren't "customers" or "clients," but "guests," because they were to be treated with the same thoughtfulness you'd show visitors to your home. You didn't wear a uniform, but a "costume," and the locker rooms were "wardrobe," because you weren't just going out to your job, you were going "onstage." The words contributed to the atmosphere that made the experience memorable for the guests.

It might all sound silly, but the mind-set that it created was extraordinary. You were put into a Disney state of mind. As soon as you walked through the gates, you did your bit and *performed*, not only because you were expected to, but also because you truly felt part of something larger than your-self. You were a part of the "cast." It was the same for the ticket takers, the cotton-candy salespeople, even the street sweepers. Disneyland's grounds were immaculate; sweepers got every cigarette butt and popcorn box in seconds. The idea was to keep it so clean people would feel uncomfortable messing it up. Looking back, it was the "broken windows" theory of crime—whereby minor violations, unaddressed, lead to major ones—decades ahead of its time.

I took all of it to heart when I began my law practice, starting with wardrobe and sets. I asked myself: What was the environment I need to create? If I were a client, how would I like my lawyer to dress?

I decided on cuff links, white shirts, suits or nice sport coats, and regimental striped ties. I made that my lawyer cos-tume and the stylistic template for the entire practice, from the other lawyers to the secretaries and receptionists.

More important, everyone understood that our clients, no matter how the rest of the world perceived them or even how they regarded themselves, were honored guests, and they were to be made to feel welcome in every possible way.

In designing my office, I tried multiple combinations of chairs and sat in all of them to see how things would look to my guests from various perspectives. And while I wanted the chairs to *look* inviting, I didn't want them to *be* all that comfortable, since I didn't necessarily want anyone staying more than fifteen or twenty minutes because of the folks waiting to see me.

My own chair, behind my desk, was elevated slightly—not throne-like, but enough to unconsciously enhance the sense that I was in control. The items on top of my desk were sim-ilarly chosen to send a message. My most important prop was the scale of justice in the corner, which differed from traditional ones in a key respect: in one pan was a tiny gavel, in the other a miniature law book; the scales were perfectly balanced. "Listen," I'd tell prospective clients, "the law is important, and so is the judge. But"—as I tipped the scales with my finger—"the lawyer you choose to sit beside you in the courtroom is more important than anything else." I know, it sounds corny—but it was very effective.

Starting out, I needed to come on strong, since I was twenty-five and looked twenty-one. It's the same reason I didn't hang my degrees on the wall; I sure as heck wasn't about to advertise I'd only been a lawyer for six months or a year.

When I got into the courtroom, it was, per Disney, my stage. I want to give not just a satisfying performance, but an *entertaining* one. So it was always important to let the jury know right up front that this was my show, my theater, my room, and I'm comfortable here.

One of the quickest ways to take ownership of a room was by moving furniture around, since in a home that's something only the owner would dare do. I'd show up early, before the judge came in and the jury was seated, and move the podium just slightly out of position, maybe three or four feet. Then afterward, when the jury was seated and the judge announced, "Mr. Giles, you may now voir dire," I'd pop out of my seat and immediately grab the lectern and move it back to the right place. As far as the jury is concerned, I'm putting it where I want it, because it's *my room.*

I was always looking for those little performance-enhancing edges. I never wanted to be caught short or embarrassed. Even sitting at home, watching a comedian bomb on Johnny Carson, it would make my skin crawl. When I stood up on my stage, I wanted the jury to mentally relax in their Barcaloungers and think, "Man, this guy's gonna put on a great show."

Of course, after Fred Douglas, that part of my life was done. So there I was, thirty-four years old, with no idea what I was going to do next. I did have an agreement with Richard Pryor to handle a number of things after he set himself on fire—his lawsuits, his finances, his marriage troubles, his career mayhem—giving him a quarter of my time for $250,000 a year. But I also knew that if I did the job right, I'd have everything resolved in two years and work my way out of the job.

On the one hand, I was nervous, since I had no idea what I'd do next. Everything about me to that point had been about being a criminal defense lawyer, and I was walking away at the top of my game. Moreover, since I was the one who'd generated most of the business, I was leaving nothing of value behind and received nothing for my interest in the firm. Eventually, the firm I'd worked so hard to build dissolved.

On the other hand, I really had no choice, since I was done representing bad people.

Still, I swore that the next business I built would not depend entirely on me. If I got run over by a truck, I'd hope that people would miss me, and come to the funeral, and say nice things, but I did not want the company to lose one dollar in value.

It is now 1983. I happen to pick up *Fortune* magazine and notice a line on the cover: "What's the most valuable franchise in America? Look inside, you'll be surprised." So, I flip it open expecting it to be MacDonald's or Taco Bell or some other fast-food chain. But instead it says . . . a Toyota dealership.

Toyota??!!

At that time, the only Japanese car anyone knew anything about was the Datsun (now Nissan) 240Z, because it was a neat little sports car. But the Japanese didn't really make cars, they made TVs and bad movies.

Toyota???

I'd never given a second's thought to a car dealership, and sure as heck not a *Japanese* car dealership. Besides which, I'd never really been a car guy, not like a lot of kids in Southern California, who spent their formative years taking apart engines and making like their hero James Dean, challenging other cars at stoplights. My cars at the time were a Rolls and a Ferrari, but I'd gotten them mostly for show, to impress clients.

But Toyota?

Yet as it happened, there was a tiny Toyota dealership nearby, and its owner was looking to sell. It was in a not-so-great area of downtown Garden Grove; one small building, no real showroom, selling thirty-five cars a month, with maybe fifty cars on the lot total, new and used. Of the 1,200 Toyota dealerships in the United States at the time, Garden Grove Toyota was number 1,150.

But you know what? It was making money.

Since, as a condition of the sale, the Toyota parent company required at least one of the buyers to know what the hell he was doing, I hired an actual car guy to be general manager and gave him a piece of the action.

While we were working on the sales contracts, we learned someone in the Garden Grove municipal government had an out-of-left-field idea. The city owned a narrow strip of land alongside the Garden Grove Freeway, one of the most heavily traveled freeways in the state, rendering it all but useless. They had an interesting notion: what if all the downtown auto dealerships relocated there, making for easy comparative shopping for consumers and increased tax dollars for the city?

The idea provoked only sarcastic grins. Why would anyone want to be right next to the competition?

But I was about to be a newbie in the business. Not only had I not absorbed the conventional wisdom, I was instinctively suspicious of it. So much in life is counterintuitive. Slow down your golf swing and the ball will go further! Turn in the direction of the skid! Move next to your competition and you will sell more cars! Why not? All I could see, which wasn't hard, was all this traffic zooming by on the freeway; that, and the fact the city was selling the property at fifty cents a square foot, when it was easily worth four times that.

The land aspect just sweetened the deal, and I jumped at it. Two years later, in October, 1985, Garden Grove Toyota opened alongside the freeway exit, and the place took off like a shot! I mean *overnight*. By the time I sold, we were the fifth-largest Toyota dealer in the world, selling 1,100 cars a month.

And, yes, within a few months, everyone else had also moved alongside the freeway. Thus was born one of America's first auto malls. Turns out being next to the competition helped everyone sell more cars.

Toyota made it almost impossible not to succeed. Back in Japan, they'd developed the automobile dealership of the future, featuring all sorts of innovations that today we take for granted—the vast showrooms designed to ideally showcase the cars, the automotive care center with cutting-edge technologies—and our facility immediately put everyone else's in town to shame.

In one of those vast cultural shifts, at that moment Americans by the millions were learning what is now common wisdom worldwide: Toyota makes a fantastic automobile. I sold my Rolls and the Ferrari and started driving a Camry myself, initially mainly to support the product—but, damn, all you had to do was not forget to put gas in those things, and they'd run forever. Forget water or oil, they'd keep going anyway.

At the time, the yen was 250–1 to the dollar—it's now 1.05–1—so not only was Toyota making the best car, but we were selling it for a price that struck people as ridiculously affordable. Meanwhile, we were paying zero up front, since

Me at age 29 at a press conference. *(Photo courtesy of the author)*

This is a picture taken of me working late one night in 1991 when I was Chairman of Pacific National Bank. *(Photo courtesy of the author)*

Me Being a Jerk and a Hero—The first picture is from a newspaper where I apparently was giving speeches before legal groups entitled "How to Make Crime Pay." I know, pretty damn obnoxious. I was clearly bragging about how lucrative our practice was. I do not remember this and it shocks my conscience. The second picture will make you feel a little better about me. In 1978 Mary Vincent was hitchhiking and was picked up by a guy named Larry Singleton. He raped her, then cut off her arms with an axe, and left her in the California desert to die. She didn't, he was arrested and sent to prison. Later she applied for orthopedic help from the State of California's Victims of Violent Crimes Act. The state refused to help her because she was a resident of Nevada and just hitchhiking across California when she was abducted. I was outraged, took her case pro bono, and we beat the crap out of California both publicity wise as well as in the court room. As a result, the laws related to assisting victims in California were changed.

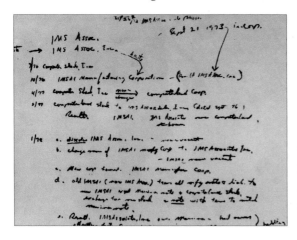

The famous "Bowman Memo" from the William Millard "Computerland" trial in 1987. *(Photo courtesy of the author)*

Martin Luther King III, Coretta Scott King, and me at Easter dinner with the family in 1984 after services at Ebenezer Baptist Church. *(Photo courtesy of the author)*

Zindzi Mandela, me, and Winnie Mandela in Johannesburg, South Africa, in 1985. *(Photo courtesy of the author)*

Me, Richard Pryor, and Armstrong Williams being welcomed by President Ronald Reagan to the White House. *(Photos courtesy of the Reagan Presidential Library)*

The head of Toyota worldwide and his entourage, visiting my dealership and announcing it was the most beautiful dealership in the world.

In 1994, I'd just received the Horatio Alger Award and the Orange County Register ran this photo of me looking at a photo of myself from when I was six years old in Cuba, Missouri. *(Photo courtesy of the author)*

First: Jeff and Cindy Reeter (Jeff was Campaign Finance Chair), Candy and Ben Carson, and Kalli and myself in my Houston home one month before Ben and I parted ways. **Second:** In preparation for the Carson campaign we traveled to Israel on a State Visit. This is Candy Carson, Kalli, and me on the Sea of Galilee. **Third:** Kalli and me addressing the crowd at our home during an early fundraiser for Ben. **Fourth:** Armstrong Williams, Kalli, and me in Jerusalem. **Fifth:** Kalli and me met with Wounded Warriors at the center for veterans who had amputee injuries. I was working on our policy positions for the Carson campaign regarding veterans and how the current US policies were insufficient and needed to change. *(Photos courtesy of the author)*

Our daughter had a close friend in undergraduate school. In their senior year (2014) he announced he was gay and his family pulled his trust and disowned him. David was a great kid and we had him move in with us for a year. I then helped get him into a special finance Masters program at Johns Hopkins. He also spoke perfect Spanish and I asked him to handle a matter for me at our home in Puerto Vallarta. While there he met a wonderful young man named Mario. David got his Masters and a great job in DC at the Department of the Treasury, Mario came to the US and started a dance studio, and the two decided to get married in 2016. David is Jewish and Mario is Catholic. They could not get a priest or rabbi to perform the ceremony. In DC anyone can get a license to marry someone and Kalli encouraged me to get a license. The picture is of me performing the marriage ceremony. The tough part was, David wanted key portions to be done in Hebrew and Mario could only speak Spanish. I speak neither, but I performed the ceremony all in Hebrew and Spanish. I was less nervous trying death penalty murder cases than I was performing that marriage between two wonderful human beings. *(Photo courtesy of the author)*

My family—**First:** My mom, LaDon Giles Hix, and me when she was 75 years old. She was an extraordinary lady who was beautiful inside and out. **Second:** Me, Keller, and Kalli on vacation in the mountains. He is now a stage actor in Seattle, Washington. **Third:** Me, our daughter Lauren, my mom, and Kalli at Lauren's graduation from Pepperdine University in 2014. **Fourth:** Me and Lauren after her college graduation next to the picture of me on the wall as Law School Alumni of the Year in 1992. **Fifth:** Me and Kalli during Christmas in Houston. **Sixth:** This photo of Kalli hiking alone in Colorado reminds me of how independent and strong she is, and yet how much I love and want to protect her. *(Photos courtesy of the author)*

the bank fully financed each car, and while the industry average was for a dealership to sell the car and pay off the bank in sixty days (called the "flooring line"), we were paying off in a day and a half. And that was only because it took us that long to get the cars off the dock, into the dealership, wash them, pinstripe them, and deliver them to the client. When the trucks carrying our cars came off the freeway, cars would actually be following them to the dealership. *Everything* was presold; you couldn't get enough Toyotas. And because we had this new store, in this prime location, Japan gave us a special allocation.

Then there were the extended warranties. We were getting them for seventy-five dollars apiece, and, I swear, the salesmen could've sold them for three thousand; we finally had to limit it to seven hundred and fifty dollars each.

And, again, it's not like those cars required much maintenance in the first place.

It was as close as I've ever come to having a printing press for money.

In this realm, as in every one since, I used the Disney model in creating the ideal sales environment. In those days, car salesmen wore wild pants and unmatched sport coats; ours wore the suits and ties of serious professionals. And no sunglasses, since it was important they be able to talk to our guests literally eye to eye. Indeed, the entire experience was designed to minimize pressure. As soon as they walked in, our guests—again, not customers—were offered coffee and told to take their time looking around; and, in the event they had small kids to distract them, we had another as-yet unheard-of feature: a play area, with a wonderfully warm woman supervising. Words created an image, the image created an environment, and the environment—as if by alchemy—manifested success.

A year or so after we started, Toyota offered its top fifty dealers in the world, the owners and their wives, an all-expense-paid trip to Toyota City in Japan to introduce that year's new line. *Impressive* doesn't begin to express it! This was the Disney mentality writ large. The factory floor was so clean you could've eaten off it, and at break time, instead of a whistle, there were gentle chimes and slowly dimming lights.

In every respect, the employer-employee relationship was grounded in mutual respect and absolute trust. It hardly needs to be said that the robotics in the factory were miles ahead of anything we had in the States at that time, but what was startling is that most of the innovations were ideas of the employees on the floor. They'd implemented 750 employee suggestions in the past year alone—that's two a day, *implemented*—for, as at Disney, they saw themselves not as employees, but team members. So, they had confidence that the technological advances would not cost them their jobs, but rather they'd be placed elsewhere in the operation.

On the factory floor there was a scoreboard with three numbers: the number of cars expected to have been produced by that point that day, the number of cars they'd actually produced, and the percentage. The entire time we were there, they were running at 102–105 percent. We were told that every once in a while, a shift would end its day at less than 100 percent—in which case, as a matter of pride, all the workers would remain on their own time to get up to 100 percent.

I sold the dealership when it was still going great guns. Why? Maybe it was my ADD kicking in, but for all our success, I knew in my bones I just wasn't a car guy. And the one thing I did know about the auto business is that it's highly volatile, and even very successful dealerships can crash and burn in a down cycle. I definitely didn't want to live in terror of getting stuck with five hundred cars gleaming out there in the Southern California sunshine, with interest piling up on every one of them.

And by then the yen was down to 150–1, 60 percent of what it had been.

Garden Grove Toyota is still successful today (I sold it to my brother-in-law—a great businessman and a real car guy), but now it's selling six hundred cars a month, still very successful but a little more than half of what we were selling thirty years ago, primarily because of the shifting value of the yen.

Let's put it this way: It was my first business after I left criminal law, and to this day it is the only one wherein I bought at exactly the right time (the bottom) and sold at exactly the right time (the top). There are several different kinds of people who succeed in the car business, and I fell under the category "Lucky Duck."

But in addition to everything else, the experience confirmed my faith in the Disney model. I'm sometimes asked what I'd do if I could, by fiat, address the problems of the American economy; and, while my answer is glib, it's also honest: run it with the same scrupulous attention to detail, honesty, and—for want of a better term—American can-do-ism as Disney would have back in the day.

CHAPTER SEVEN

The Power of Words

Be straight with yourself, because excuses are a dead end

Again—and this cannot be emphasized too strongly!—opportunities exist in our lives every day in multiple ways. We just have to align our vision and our words to be able to find them—and not flinch when they find us.

This demands calm, perspective, and, above all, the capacity to recognize and accurately assess the opportunity at hand.

To not simply look, but to *see*. To not simply listen, but to *hear*.

We tend to take language for granted. In fact, words are the foundation of human existence. It is words that shape our vision, make us cry or laugh, alter our behavior, transform our lives. It is words, properly chosen and deployed, that enable us to move forward. It is words that create possibilities and opportunities.

Nobody knew that better than Walt Disney—and Werner Erhard, a close friend, the founder of est (Erhard Seminar Training), and one of the thought leaders of our times.

I had never attended est, and in its heyday in the late 1970s and early 1980s, I had heard some of the crazy rumors: that this guy Erhard was filling up the Cow Palace in San Francisco for his seminars, harassing attendees about how they should live their lives and not letting them go to the bathroom. Except for the sold-out courses, nothing could have been further from the truth.

I kept running into people I admired who'd been through the program, often highly successful businesspeople, and everyone similarly described it as "transformative." Over and over, I heard variations on the same theme, that est was helping them be better. Better with family. Better with partners. Better with employees. Better *people*. Werner had zero interest in telling others how to live their lives. All he asked of others was to be honest in how they viewed themselves and how they articulated that vision. The essential tenet of est was that we are the cause of our life direction. Our lives are vessels, and how we fill them is, to a surprisingly large degree, up to us. Be honest, especially with yourself, don't use your words to deceive or obfuscate. Don't blame your problems on your parents, siblings, boss, or life circumstances. You have an enormous say in who you are. If you do not like who you are—change it! If you want your life to be full and meaningful—do something about it now and make it so.

By now, you know that I have no problem stating my opinion about almost anything, and that goes double for my feelings about Werner and Landmark Worldwide, which I discuss later in this chapter. But it's also important to me to be clear that while Werner and the folks at Landmark have been a major influence on me, it is not my intent to imply that all of my views are shared by them. There are enormous similarities, which I will emphasize, but I am also my own person on my own journey with my own perspectives. The point being is if you have a disagreement with something I have said, the problem is with me and not Werner or Landmark.

As Werner says in his own words, "At each moment of our life and under any circumstances, you and I possess within ourselves, at every moment of our lives and under all circumstances, the power to transform the quality of our lives."

My reaction? "Wow, that's what I believe, but I've never heard it expressed so elegantly in words."

Little wonder I hit it off so well with est's creator, since in my mind my beliefs aligned so closely with his—not just my general worldview, but with so many of its particulars. What was most appealing was Werner's absolute clarity. He put into words, and made accessible to multitudes, concepts I'd felt on my own, without having consciously expressed them. His thinking was brilliant—but his use of words was otherworldly. His words not only were magical, but also made you think.

- "You want power, treat what you give your word to like it was sacred. Being a man or woman of integrity creates a new world—a world without messes. Integrity for an object, system, person, or other human entity (such as an organization) is the condition of being whole and complete. Integrity for a person (or other human entity) is a matter of that person's word, or that entity's word."

- "To be a man or a women of integrity, one's word must be whole and complete. However, you will not always be good for your word. As soon as you become aware that you will not keep your word, you maintain your integrity by acknowledging to those who were counting on your word that you will not keep your word. Then say by when you will keep that word or that you never will, and do what you can to clean up any mess caused by not keeping your word."

- "There is power in being authentic. Being authentic is being and acting consistent with who you hold yourself out to be for others, and who you hold yourself to be for yourself. The beginning of authenticity is being *authentic* about your *inauthenticity*."
- "It is not enough to *want* a better life, you have to actually state in vivid detail what that looks like. It is that articulated future reality from which your brain generates your being and action in the present."

If someone had asked me earlier about my life philosophy and why I thought it worked, I'd probably have said something about loyalty and keeping my promises. But I'd never have gotten so directly to the heart of it, and maybe entirely overlooked the bit about cleaning up the messes we make. That's the part that's all too easy, and morally convenient, to miss. But Werner rarely misses anything in what he investigates and questions.

At the time we met, Werner was under siege from multiple directions. Here was a great man doing great work, but the work he was doing was, at the time, new and different. Being different can create jealousy and misunderstanding, and so it was in the case of Werner Erhard. The same media that had earlier extolled him for his insights now tried to make a case for fraud. He was wrongly and inappropriately being targeted by the IRS. But far, far worse, *60 Minutes* would run a segment in which he was wrongfully accused of abusing one of his daughters. All of these accusations were false, but how do you un-ring those bells?

How? By destroying the lies one at a time.

Although the IRS came after him with unconscionable ferocity, they were completely wrong, and their errors ended up causing them to have to pay Werner what was at that time a historically high damage award.

When examining the other attacks it became increasingly apparent that Scientology was behind his other troubles. Scientology has vast financial resources, and true believers in high places, and its founder, L. Ron Hubbard, despised Werner, ridiculously believing est poached his adherents. Indeed, Hubbard had formally declared Erhard "Fair Game," which in Scientology-speak meant that any member could lie or do illegal acts to destroy Werner and be forgiven. Meanwhile, Scientologists were filing bogus lawsuits against Werner on a regular basis and trying to create negative press. Scientology, the original purveyors of fake news, was out to destroy one of the most extraordinary persons I had ever met.

As I set about defending Werner, my first task was to get him out of the line of fire so he wouldn't keep getting served with papers and tied up in depositions. So, I sent him down to my place in Puerto Vallarta for a couple of months, and from there he went to Japan—the Japanese and other cultures in Asia have a special appreciation for his work—and he ended up living there for a number of years.

Now, able to operate freely, we go on the offensive. It takes some time, but eventually we're able to get all the lawsuits dismissed. Far more important, we establish that the newspaper reporter who originally broke the "abuse" story was connected to Scientology, and that he'd promised the daughter certain financial rewards for the fictional story. The truth has a way of exposing itself, and the daisy chain of lies unraveled. After the claim was proven to be false, CBS took the unusual step of decertifying the *60 Minutes* segment, removing it from their archive and leaving in its place a notice that they no longer stand by the accuracy of their report in the broadcast. Vindication was finally and completely achieved.

I feel compelled to also mention that it has been my experience that true character and a valid set of principles emerge, not in good times, but when things are at their darkest. Throughout all of the stress and craziness of the years of attack, Werner never altered who he was or what he stood for. He was a rock! That, as much as anything else, causes me to be able to say that Werner Erhard is the real thing.

But since Werner was the glue who'd held things together, in his absence the business had gone on life support. As if that weren't bad enough, there was a war brewing between the company's top executives and the operation staff and Forum Leaders (those on the ground who actually organized and ran the programs and otherwise made the company and its programs functional).

From abroad, Werner gave me complete authority to sell the company and work out a solution. He made it clear he didn't care about the money; his interest was in ensuring that the work—his well-thought-out principles and ideas—not die. I met with both sides in the dispute, individually and together, and in the end, I selected the operational staff and Forum Leaders. As naive as they were business-wise, they'd grown up with the est technology and had lived it, while the other guys were ready to fundamentally change the company's business model, turning it into something more akin to Tony Robbins's operation.

The company was renamed Landmark, and the primary program was now The Landmark Forum; but, in part to further assure continuity, Werner's much younger brother, Harry Rosenberg, became CEO. Eventually the name changed again, to Landmark Worldwide, but it's been over a quarter century now, and Harry Rosenberg has emerged as one of the best CEOs I've ever seen. Under his care, team-building skills, and partnership with extraordinary department heads, Landmark today has offices all over the world, and incredible licensees that pay a royalty to use the intellectual technologies. People inside Landmark behave in remarkable ways, unlike those in any other business with which I've ever been associated. If someone makes a mistake, they own up to it before anyone else even notices. It's personal responsibility to the nth degree at every level, up and down the chain, and it is a foolproof recipe for success. At Landmark, integrity is more than just a word, it is a way of living.

I love the folks at Landmark, and I was honored when in 2000 they asked me to become chairman.

Today the company is what's known as an ESOP, meaning it's entirely owned by the employees. As chairman, my sole responsibilities are to attend a handful of meetings a year and make myself available as needed to consult with Harry and the other execs on any legal or business matters that come up.

As for Werner, he is now recognized as the exceptional thought leader he truly is and is now lecturing at major universities around the world. He continues to examine the nature of human intellect and uses the power of words to help others create and re-create their lives through the articulation of words that describe the world they wish to live into. He references it as the "world to word" view, a concept wherein the world aligns itself and your future with the words you carefully select to describe that future.

But there are still detractors, and if someone writes a misinformed story that wrongfully refers to Werner as some kind of cult leader, or compares est to some cult, I'm on their ignorant ass pronto, getting a retraction.

And Landmark continues to bring good into many, many lives. Indeed, all these years later, it remains the job that leaves me surest I'm contributing to the well-being of the world. I cherish my relationship with Werner, Harry, and dozens of executives and Forum leaders who perform at incredible levels of competence.

Words have power. It is not for nothing that it is said that you are only as good as your word. I believe with certainty that there is a point in the lives of every member of the 15 percent where the only thing they had was their word. Even today, many would say it is still their most valuable asset.

CHAPTER EIGHT

Remaining Flexible— Current Best Idea

Follow your instincts *and* your passions

There is a phrase I like to use in my companies to promote creative thinking: Current Best Idea. It was coined by one of my best friends, William Millard, and is shorthand for that mix of flexibility and out-of-the-box thinking that informs the behavior of those in the 15 percent across professions and geographical boundaries. You don't just arrive at one idea, tie a ribbon around it, and congratulate yourself on a job well done. To the contrary, even when things are going well, you're constantly looking to hit on a *new* Current Best Idea, one that will more effectively and efficiently advance your business, your career, yourself.

Every potential CBI, no matter how seemingly unorthodox, merits a full and fair hearing. With enough brainstorming, there's no knowing where it will lead, since good things

99

routinely emerge from the nuttiest-sounding ideas. At meetings, I'll often suggest we do a mind dump. "Don't worry if a notion makes sense, because who knows, it might lead to a new concept, and that will grow into an unbelievable idea."

In short, you're letting your associates know up front that you're in this together—and that even the worst idea won't be held against them.

I know it was a form of game show that was trying to entertain, but when I used to watch Donald Trump on *The Apprentice*, I thought the show's guiding premise was flawed. If something goes wrong in business, you get ahead not by taking responsibility and finding a way to fix it, but by pointing fingers and shifting blame. It's precisely the opposite of the idea that innovative thinking is to be encouraged and rewarded.

Still, the Current Best Idea concept does come with an important caveat, which has to do with *which* ideas to pursue.

Successful businesses are born of passion and follow-through, so it's vital to know going in if what's on the table is the right fit for your personality and style. True, there are some for whom the sole consideration is dollars and cents; if they're convinced the bottom line is right, they'll move ahead without hesitation or qualm on *any* project.

But I suspect I'm more typical in this respect. Of all the businesses I've been involved with over the years, I think back most fondly on the ones that most interested me. I loved working on them because they were *fun*; they hit my pleasure center. And it's no coincidence that they were usually very lucrative.

While I lucked out big-time in the automobile business, I was also lucky to get out before my lack of knowledge came back to bite. And in that case, I at least met the minimum standard of being able to see myself as a customer. Hey, maybe I wasn't a car guy, but I had *bought* cars.

By depressing, and let's hope instructive, contrast, here's what happened when I found myself in the carpet pad business. Not carpets—at least that might have been occasionally interesting—but the pads underneath. I bought this company out of bankruptcy for a fraction of what the equipment and factory were worth, so it sounded like a can't-miss deal. But the fact is, I never really got the business, or wanted to bother learning it. And by the time I'd sunk in the money needed to get it restarted, it wasn't so can't-miss anymore.

The problem, if you care (and if you don't, feel free to skip this paragraph), is that the pads were made of foam rubber, which had to be bought used and then remolded. And the primary source of scrap foam rubber in those days was, of all things, used-car seats.

Anyway, one night I'm at a big dinner party, a very elegant affair, having a terrific time, when I get called to the phone. It's the head guy down at the factory, who informs me there's a scrap rubber shortage, having to do with a rise in used-car sales, so the price is suddenly sky-high. I knew immediately it is over, and that all the money we invested is down the drain, since the big carpet pad companies are better able to absorb price cuts, and there's no way we can compete. I vividly remember walking back into the dining room, and looking at all these people having a great time, and I'm thinking, *How the heck did this happen? How did I end up the only one in this room who gives a damn about the price of scrap rubber? Or even knows there IS a price for scrap rubber?*

But, then, by way of happier contrast, there was the business I bought into while building the Toyota dealership: Pacific National Bank.

Once again, the Disney model was invaluable. As bank chairman in those days, I realized that our most important customers were not the chief executives of the companies we dealt with, but their secretaries or executive assistants, because they not only ran the CEO's lives, but before online banking they also showed up to make deposits. So, at our bank, these folks were honored guests; we were on a first-name basis with everyone, knew the names of their spouses and children, their favorite pastries, and how they took their coffee or tea. We even had personalized ceramic mugs made, with their initials embossed. It was ridiculous how successful those cups were, if for no other reason than no one else was doing it.

I absolutely loved running the bank. I'd never been particularly proud of telling people I was a car dealer, since on the descending social pecking order, it was garbagemen, car dealers, lawyers. But I loved saying I was chairman of a bank! It was empowering, it was lucrative, it was ever-changing. We were at the epicenter of everything happening financially throughout Orange County, and there were deals to be made left and right. Our loan committee met once a week, and I always looked forward to it, because anyone asking for a loan had to undress—show you their assets and tell you in detail what they were investing in. It was like a financial peep show. And the analogy is not accidental, because for someone who loves deals and numbers as much as I do, it was the ultimate turn-on. It may not have been my project, but I could still appreciate a great deal when I saw one, or spot a particularly lousy one, and wonder what the heck they were thinking. I mean, you were aware of *everything*. Obviously, I respected confidentiality, but it was still incredibly interesting knowing all this stuff.

Then, too, occasionally, an investment opportunity might walk through the door. That's how I became aware of University Copy System, which owned the rights to Canon office machines for the greater LA area. I invested six months before fax machines hit the market—in October 1985. This was another hot new product from a Japanese company, and, coming off the car business, the first thing I wanted to know is what these guys were doing with warranties. Sure enough, even in those early days, they were selling machines and making significant money on warranties. So we were immediately on the same wavelength, and when they offered me the chance to buy 45 percent of the business, I jumped at it. Sure enough, it was Toyota all over again: best product on the market, lowest price, the company going through the roof.

I also did a couple of other nice deals—land deals in Laguna Beach.

I never should have sold the bank; doing so was one of the great mistakes of my career.

It's just that in the 1990s, under President Clinton, the government introduced the Community Reinvestment Act, which basically meant you had to invest 10 percent of your portfolio into the poor neighborhoods in your region. I found this deeply offensive. We'd been buying up savings and loan assets in Newport Beach and Beverly Hills, and I had no interest in loaning into the poorer areas of greater Los Angeles. It had nothing to do with racial or wealth bias; it had everything to do with loaning to companies and people who could and would pay it back, regardless of creed or color. That's what you *do* as a bank. And, as we know, the CRA was a part of a series of policies that would lead directly to the mortgage crisis in 2008.

I was so upset, I flatly refused to play—I'd be damned if I'd let the federal government tell me who I'm going to lend to or not lend to! And the penalty, in essence, was they wouldn't let our bank purchase additional assets and continue to grow. So, I sold it.

But as always, there were ways around it, and the really smart guys in banking figured out how to give the appearance of compliance without actually putting much of their loan portfolio at risk. They came up with a better Current Best Idea. I bailed too quickly, when I should have stuck with it.

Of course, by then I was also ready to move on to the next thing, since there are always lots of Current Best Ideas in the air.

Above all, I wanted to do something internationally—had wanted to for years. When I was doing criminal law, I had a case in Montreal, and it was a total blast. My client was an American woman who'd jumped bail and fled to the United States ten years earlier, after getting arrested in Montreal with a couple of joints. Now, married with a family, she wanted to clear her record. So there I found myself, in a totally different court system. Here the other side wasn't the government, it was "the Crown," and instead of a court reporter, everything was recorded electronically. My only regret was that, as an American, they didn't make me wear the traditional wig and robe. Of course, on the upside, I also didn't have to speak French. Otherwise, my client would probably still be rotting in a Montreal jail, instead of getting off with a fine and time served.

But that taste, even if it was just Canada, was intoxicating. Now that I'd become a businessman, I wanted to be an *international* businessman, a feeling only heightened by the Toyota experience. Indeed, having closely watched the fluctuations of the yen to figure how it affected pricing on our cars, I was fascinated by currencies.

My initial thought was that I could take advantage of the relationships I'd started to build in Asia. No good. It didn't take long to see that Japan, as well as places like China and Singapore in those days, were closed systems, where the best opportunities were only for the locals.

So at thirty-nine years old, with anticipation and a fear-lessness enhanced by the experiences already under my belt, I set out to explore the world in search of possibilities. I soon landed in what was then still called West Germany, where it was impossible not to be struck by the incredible prop-erty deals available. It was like California in the mid-1960s—except back then I'd been in high school and couldn't take advantage. Also, the deutsche mark was 2.1 to the dollar, and you could get assumable mortgages for 3 percent; this at a time, starting with President Carter, when the prime rate in the United States had been as high as 21 percent, and mort-gage rates on homes were still at 8–9 percent. Even better, in Germany those mortgages were fully assumable, meaning you could sell those babies to somebody else!

So, I started buying property in Germany, and then, boom, out of the blue, the Wall comes down! Suddenly the deutsche mark is 1.4 to one, meaning I've already made back a third of what I paid for the property just on the financial exchange. With everyone now wanting to be in Germany, property val-ues start skyrocketing, and with mortgages now at 12 per-cent, I'm also cashing in on all those 3 percent assumables. I thought I'd died and gone to heaven.

Still, lucrative as it was, it wasn't quite perfect. Because, at least for me, Northern Germany just wasn't a fun place to be.

Which is how I ended up not just on the French Riviera, but in the hotel business.

I was taking a few days off, staying at a hotel in Monaco, and the concierge suggested I might enjoy having lunch at a pretty little town nearby called Eze. Though he didn't know it, it would prove the Current Best Idea of all time.

Eze was a medieval village, a thousand years old, all winding cobblestone streets and ancient alleys, untouched by time. High up a steep hill, it looms 1,300 feet over the

Mediterranean and Cap Ferrat; and at the very top, with star-tling views of the sea, stood a castle in ruin that long ago protected the town from marauding pirates.

For this Southern California boy by way of rural Missouri, it was love at first sight.

Since earliest childhood, I'd had a thing for castles. I didn't have many toys, but the ones I did have were forts or castles. I'd position the little plastic men strategically and let them have at it. Rin Tin Tin and his guys at Fort Apache against the Indians; Davy Crockett at the Alamo; Robin Hood and his Merry Men attacking the knights in their castle. So, when I'd come to Europe, it was magical seeing these things actu-ally standing there, even more impressive in real life. I could scarcely even imagine what it must be like to own one.

I was so taken with Eze, I decided I had to at least own *something* in the village. I figured it would be an ideal base; twenty minutes from Nice Airport, from which I could reach anywhere in Europe in a couple of hours. So, I booked a room in the thousand-year-old castle/hotel, Château Eza, which commands the most dramatic corner of Eze Village and is simply amazing. The former home of the Swedish royal fam-ily, the château was now transformed into a five-star hotel, complete with a Michelin-star restaurant, and a jaw-dropping view of the Côte d'Azur.

The next morning, I began my search. It proved a long and frustrating afternoon. Not only was there nothing avail-able in the village, it was clear there never would be; the same families had owned these stone houses for six hundred years, passing them on from generation to generation. Over and over, I heard variations of the same line: *"Non, monsieur, very sorry, but this house has been in the family since 1481."*

I'm back at the hotel that evening, drowning my disap-pointment over an excellent house wine and a terrific dinner, when the owner of the place stops by my table. When he finds out I'm alone, he offers to join me and orders another bottle of wine. It turns out he's a Swiss guy, named Andre Rochat, and he has a fascinating history, much of it spent running the Red Cross in the Middle East as a kind of modern Lawrence of Arabia. Among other things, when Black September—the group who'd murdered the Israeli athletes at the Munich Olympics—pulled off their next operation, taking three planes simultaneously and parking them in the Saudi desert, he was the one who'd negotiated the release of the passengers before the planes were blown up. Over the years, he said, he'd gotten chummy with the Saudi royal family, and it was through them he met the Swedish royal family, who at the time was using this castle as their summer residence, and that's how he came to own it. Just as he was thinking of returning to Europe, he learned they were looking to sell.

So, he's telling me these amazing stories, and we're drinking a lot of excellent wine, and after a while it feels like we're becoming buddies. When he asks me why I'm there, I tell him my sad story, and he says, "Well, would you be interested in buying this place?"

"Really?! I didn't know it was available."

"Well, it's not, really. But I'm sixty-seven, I've never been married, and I don't have any children, so I have no one to leave it to when I retire. So five years from now, if you're still interested, we can talk."

Then somewhere around the middle of the next bottle of wine, I get an idea. And somewhere in the middle of the bottle after that, we get out a piece of paper and sketch out a deal. I'll buy 20 percent of the hotel each of the next five years. The first 20 percent, he'll still be able to rent out those rooms when I'm not there, but I get to use them when I am. So I have my place in Eze, eventually I'll get full ownership, and in the interim he'll continue to run the hotel as he wants, keeping 100 percent of the profits.

"And at the end of five years, the sale is complete," I say, "you retire, and I take over operations."

From the start, the plan worked flawlessly. I have a place on the Côte d'Azur, with five years to get to know the operation and the employees, and to figure out what I wanted to change. The place *was,* after all, a bit cold and austere—thousand-year-old stone walls will do that—so each time I took over another 20 percent, I redecorated to add more warmth.

I assumed full ownership in 1994, keeping Andre on the board until he passed away.

Some assets bring you joy, some assets bring you pain. Château Eza is one that has given me nothing but unalloyed pleasure. I can't tell you how many dinner parties I've been to where someone will start talking about having vacationed at this fabulous hotel in the South of France, and its extraordinary restaurant, telling everyone else at the table how they absolutely have to go to this place, Château Eza—at which point I'll chime in, "Oh, I own that." And everyone turns and looks at me like I'm from Mars.

As a bonus, it's been a hugely effective tool for my other businesses. Appearances matter—anyone who denies it is a fool—and there couldn't be a better stage on which to do my thing. I know darn well that when a potential business associate walks onto the deck at Château Eza, a large part of my job is already done, because he's sold on me before I say a word. It's the greatest home-court advantage anyone could have.

We have just fourteen rooms and a forty-five-seat Michelin-Star restaurant. But we also have those amazing decks, with their breathtaking views of the sea, and between May and September, we serve 41,000 people out there. Basically, they rent a spot for an hour or two; have an ice cream, a Coke, or a glass or two of wine; and although they spend an average of just 20.2 euros apiece, multiplied by 41,000 people (figuring the cost of sales is 7 percent), it's not half bad.

My experience with Château Eza has been so fantastic, I later bought another luxury hotel, the Gran Hotel Son Net, in Majorca. It was formerly—what else?—a 16th-century fortified palace. According to Condé Nast, today it's the most romantic hotel/restaurant in Europe, and it's ranked by TripAdvisor as the number one hotel in Majorca.

All things considered, the hotels will probably wind up being the best deals I ever made. I bought both at the right time, and the property values have skyrocketed. But, most important, they've given me nothing but happiness. And our team is incredible—David Stein is a property development and marketing genius, Roger Vrignaud is the best chief financial officer I have ever known, and Robin Oodunt and Jesus Stein are excellent general managers, both loyal and trustworthy.

None of this is to say that, in considering a deal, I *ever* downplay the matter of potential profitability; if I did that, *I* wouldn't want to be in business with me, let alone anyone else.

Still, if you hooked me up to one of the lie detectors I used in my former profession, I'd probably confess there are at least a couple of deals I did for entertainment value that I'd have done even knowing there'd be a few drops of red ink at the end.

The magic club, for instance.

It was called Magic Island, a private club in Newport Beach, and by every objective standard, it was a royal pain in the neck. But magic is one of my passions. In fact, that's how I got involved with Magic Island in the first place, as a member, then buying it when it went into bankruptcy.

So, we're not talking a replay of the carpet pad experience. I had big plans for the place. My idea was to open it to the general public. I hired a friend from Disney to run it for me, and we had a great bar and high-end cuisine and put a singer in the lounge to go with the top magic acts in the country, along with all the latest technology.

But for me, the best part may have been the close-up, sleight-of-hand performances in the smaller side spaces. What they did really *was* magic.

There was one magician in particular who impressed me, Bob Albo. In his other life, he was a cancer surgeon and the most decorated letterman in the history of Cal Berkeley—sixteen letters in four years, in varsity baseball, basketball, football, and track—yet he was also the number one amateur magician and one of the best cancer surgeons in the world. You'd see this guy walk in, six foot five, with huge hands, and wonder how he could possibly have the delicacy and touch to be a top surgeon; but then you'd see him perform close up, with a deck of cards or three baseballs, and you'd know. Things would disappear into and reappear out of those huge hands so quickly it was impossible to figure out how.

Then it all went to hell. There was a fire—probably arson, though that was never proven—and the club had to be rebuilt. Then, I discovered that our insurance agent had lied when he told me we had a binder for insurance; so I then had to sue my insurance guy's insurance carrier. As a result, I reached the point where not only was the fun gone, I started to hate going to Magic Island, because the moment I walked through the door I'd be assaulted by a hundred problems.

The low point was New Year's Eve, 1990. By now the place has been rebuilt and just reopened, and my wife wants to go there to celebrate. I say no, I'd really rather not; but since I had been working a lot lately, and I want to be a good guy, I give in.

The evening starts off great. They've set aside our favorite table, and we're being left totally alone. The club is packed, several hundred people in tuxes and evening gowns, each of whom has paid a thousand dollars to be here, and never has it looked more festive.

It's maybe 10 o'clock, we're in the middle of our dinner, and after several glasses of wine, I'm more relaxed than I've been in weeks, when our manager appears and kneels beside the table.

"I've got some really bad news." Pause. "One of our valet drivers went on a joyride in a guest's car and hit somebody in a crosswalk."

"Holy crap, you've got to be kidding me!"

"It gets worse. We have no idea where the keys are to any of the cars they parked."

I can only look around at all these wonderful people in black tie, having a ball, who don't know they can't leave tonight in their cars—or even *find* them, since we didn't have a parking lot and the cars are parked on the streets of Newport Beach.

It turns out the rogue valet put the keys in the trunk of the car he was joyriding in, which has now been impounded by the police. Of course, we only discover this later. Right now, our problem is explaining this to these people—that and finding enough limousines at 10:30 on New Year's Eve to get them all home. Then, the next morning, after we'd figured out where the keys were, we had to pick them all up again, see if they could find their keys among the hundreds in the pile, and drive them around the streets of Newport Beach until they find their car.

Thank God the pedestrian survived. And, amazingly, I was able to stay out of the lawsuits that followed, since the valet wasn't our employee, but part of a service we'd hired. Still, this wasn't, shall we say, the best possible publicity for the club. Not long after, I sold it to the employees.

All in all, maybe the most miserable night of my life.

So isn't it strange, looking back on it now, that the first thing I remember when I think of the magic club was the joy of owning it? That and the fact that we hired a young girl, nineteen years old, as an office assistant, and thirty years later that girl, Kristen Blackford, is my chief of staff. She is so efficient I often explain that she is both my left and right arm. She is simply amazing, and I do not know how I could run my life without her!

As an investment philosophy, it is good to remember that we are all human. We invest sometimes with our wallet and sometimes with our heart. But either way, a vital ingredient of success is doing it with our eyes open, always evaluating changing circumstances to ensure flexibility. As in baseball where a great shortstop is always on the balls of his feet, ready to move right or left, one must consistently be nimble in business. For those in the 15 percent, this is second nature. They have been doing it their entire lives. Everything—and I mean everything—is a potential Current Best Idea.

CHAPTER NINE

"Nothing" Can Be Everything

**You never know where something
will lead until you follow it**

I once had a constitutional law professor who'd tell us that no matter what we went on to do as lawyers, we'd always be dealing with constitutional issues, they were embedded in cases large and small—and yet, he added, he ran across lawyers in practice thirty years who assured him they'd never had a single constitutional issue in any of their cases. Of course, it wasn't true; they were just blind to the obvious.

It's the same with opportunity. Millions of people go through life thinking they've been unlucky and have never had a shot at getting ahead in life. But really what happened— they didn't have the capacity to recognize it.

Those in the 15 percent may have problems, but that's not one of them. Because there are opportunities in every lifetime.

And if you're in the right frame of mind, they're all over the place.

My first wife used to complain that we didn't spend enough time together, because I was forever chasing after some shiny new possibility. I couldn't deny it.

"What's the point," she'd say, "it's a nothing thing."

But there she was wrong. Nothing is not nothing. Nothing can be everything. There's no way of knowing where something will lead until it's been closely examined and assessed. The greatest results often come from the smallest beginnings.

Take how I met William Millard, for thirty-five years now one of my closest friends.

William is remarkable. Having worked with IBM in the 1950s, by the early 1960s he was one of the most knowledgeable computer minds in the world. He wired the cities of Oakland and San Francisco before anyone thought it possible. After the Kennedy assassination he helped law enforcement develop the P.I.N. (Police Information Network). In the early 1970s his company, IMSAI, invented the first personal computer as we know it—the IMSAI 8080. The problem was that technology was moving so fast, by the time he'd completed production, the machine was nearly obsolete. As a result, when IMSAI was shuttered in 1976, William started a company he called "ComputerLand." Selling the best manufactured computers of the day, it became the largest retailer of computers in the world for two decades. In 1984, *Forbes* called him the "Instant Billionaire."

Yet, by 1985, William's world was in turmoil. He had two lawsuits pending. While his antagonists in the suits were different individuals, the actions were identical, and in fact pending in front of the same Alameda County judge. William had hired Edward Bennett Williams's firm out of Washington, D.C., to defend him. Ed Williams, arguably America's best-ever lawyer, consulted on the case, but Ray Berman was the trial lawyer assigned by the firm. Berman was experienced, tough, and formerly represented Jimmy Hoffa.

Nonetheless, the first trial went terribly wrong. The jury returned a verdict for $141.5 million for the plaintiff against the company and Millard in punitive damages, then a California record, plus an award of 45 percent of ComputerLand, worth hundreds of millions of dollars.

To make matters worse, William still had the second case pending in the same courtroom before the same judge. The plaintiff's lawyers were licking their chops.

When William sent his troops out to find a new trial lawyer, they eventually contacted me. I politely explained that I had retired from the law and why. However, I did offer to speak to Mr. Millard, if only to offer advice on what kind of trial lawyer he should choose. Why did I do that, knowing a meeting would take a whole day at a time I was knee-deep in the auto dealership, the bank, the copier company, and a million other things? Simple. Who knew where it might lead?

So I flew to Oakland, and William and I had lunch. As I began to understand the mistakes that had been made in the first trial, I could see that this remarkable man found himself bear-trapped by a legal system I knew all too well.

Over the next three decades I would learn to highly regard William's ability to focus, and even in that first meeting I could not help but notice how intently he listened to my advice, writing everything down. Still, I had to emphasize I was retired from the law, and when I left I figured I'd probably never see him again.

But a week later, his office called requesting another meeting. Once again, I flew to Oakland, and again his driver picked me up. Only this time, instead of going to his house, he drove to the private airport where Mr. Millard's private Falcon was

warming up to take off. Told to board the plane, the next
thing I knew we were wheels up on the way to Boston. Fifteen
minutes into the flight, the stewardess walked me to the rear
of the plane. A door opened into a compartment set up as an
office for William. Greeting me, he handed me a first-class
ticket from Boston back to Los Angeles, and invited me to
join him for lunch.

He began by saying how much by now he absolutely hated
lawyers—and the fact that I'd had the good sense to quit the
law meant I was the lawyer for him.

I say I'm flattered, which I very much am, but I didn't
think so. My own experience had been as soul-searing as his,
and though I'm still getting lots of calls from would-be clients, that door was closed.

Millard brushed that aside. "Listen," he said, "I have a prop-
osition . . . ," and then, at 36,000 feet, he made me an incredible
offer. Would I be willing to put together a small firm, personally hiring everyone from lawyers to secretaries, that would
have the sole purpose of preparing and trying the second case?

That got my attention. A "dream team" a decade before
the term had been coined, totally under my control, yet wholly
financed by the client. Every trial lawyer's fantasy scenario.
And of course, I would not be representing my usual type
of client. I would represent him and his cause—a man and a
position I could believe in.

"It wouldn't be cheap," I said, musing aloud. "We're
talking at least three lawyers, a couple of paralegals, a good
investigator. Figure $40,000 a month in overhead alone for
as long as it takes." In 1985, that was not just chickenfeed.

"And how much for you?"

"Probably another $40,000 a month." I paused, consider-
ing. "And if I win, I'd want a bonus of a million."

"What does winning mean?"

"That you won't have to give the people suing you a penny."

It was the first time I'd seen him smile.

"Look," I put it to him at Logan Airport, before boarding a flight back to California, "you seem like a good guy and this is incredibly intriguing. But I don't really know you. Give me three weeks to do my own investigation, and if I think you're in the right, I'll take the case. If not, no hard feelings."

He gave me full access to ComputerLand's records and personnel, and I reviewed the transcripts from the first trial. It was an easy call: there was no doubt he'd gotten well and truly screwed. Quite simply, the plaintiff's attorney in the first case, a flamboyant, canny veteran named Herb Hafif, had run circles around Millard's guy.

How ironic that I had to leave the practice of law in order to meet the perfect client and represent the ideal cause.

Since it's probably a year before our case is to come to trial, I use the time to immerse myself in ComputerLand's culture, learning the cast of characters and sitting in on top-level meetings. Since I keep my mouth shut, after a while people start to consider me safe, and neutral, someone they can confide in; and in a company as unsettled as this one with a huge verdict from the first trial threatening its very existence and where no one knows what's coming next, everyone is bursting with things to say.

One huge problem is Millard's management style. As chairman, he is so forbidding a presence that around him even corporate lawyers and top executives clam up. His relationship with his longtime CEO is especially fraught, so much so I'm picking up rumblings there's a coup afoot. Worse, it appears that the real power behind it is Herb Hafif, the lawyer who, after creaming Millard in the first trial, now controls a hefty share of ComputerLand's assets. Hafif's all about ego and power—years ago he ran for governor, finishing sixth in a field of six—and having come to despise Millard during the trial, he wants nothing more than to unseat the founder and chairman and take over the company.

Worse still, one of my longtime friends may be among the conspirators, while another person I care deeply about, Ron Helm, is maintaining loyalty to Millard.

Learning all this, I agonized over what to do. Both friends are good guys, while Millard is just a client, whom I still address as "Mr. Millard."

Still, there is no question that as his lawyer, I have to let him know.

I was sitting at my desk, literally looking for his phone number, when my secretary buzzed that William Millard is on the phone.

He sounds like I've never heard him before, almost distraught. "Listen, Terry," he says, "I know we don't know each other well, but I'm really down. Something's going on, and I've got a really uneasy feeling. Are you available to sit down and talk?"

"Well, it's amazing, I was just going to give you a call. And, yeah, we need to talk."

The next morning, I flew up to Oakland for what was a truly extraordinary meeting. I told William everything I knew, and what I expected to happen, none of it good. But, to my surprise, he took it all in with seeming calm. More, and this ran counter to everything in his makeup, he accepted his full share of responsibility for what had led to this juncture.

He then granted me authority to approach his adversaries and work out a settlement—even if that meant his surrendering the chairmanship.

It was a conversation that forever cemented my relationship with William Millard. The trust on both sides has been absolute and irrevocable ever since.

There's no time to waste. It's Saturday morning, and the CEO and the other chief conspirators are set to finalize their deal with Hafif on Monday.

I'm able to track down the CEO and my friend at a local golf club; in the midst of a round, they're startled to see me, in suit and tie, walking toward them down the fairway. At my side, to confirm I've been granted the authority I claim, is Millard's daughter. We repair to the clubhouse, and I tell them they no longer need Herb Hafif to get the power they seek in the company, and, then and there, we begin hammering out a settlement. Millard will indeed step aside, transferring control to his executives—with some important conditions.

With that situation stabilized, I shift my focus to preparing for the lawsuit. Fortunately, in light of the other's side's success in the first trial, I have the advantage of pretty much knowing what they'll throw at me, and there's one witness in particular whose testimony we definitely need to counter: a lawyer named Bowman, who started with Millard at IMSAI and later moved with him to ComputerLand. He claimed, under oath, that the deal with the plaintiffs was designed from the get-go to protect William and screw the employees.

It was absolutely devastating testimony, and the primary reason for the huge punitive damages.

Millard, for his part, maintained that, in fact, he had explicitly instructed the lawyer to see that the agreement was "done right," and fair to all concerned; and, indeed, once it had been drafted, he'd had Bowman draw up a diagram showing exactly how the deal was meant to work.

While this document would counter Bowman's testimony and destroy his credibility, no such diagram had been unearthed, and even Millard's own lawyers apparently came to regard it as a figment of his imagination.

However, I trusted William's explanation for two reasons. First, I found William's integrity to be sterling. Second, Bowman had a reason to lie. After he quit at ComputerLand, the plaintiffs in the first case gave him a piece of the action—if he testified for them in the manner that he had.

All IMSAI's old files were now in storage in an Oakland warehouse, but William swore that Bowman's memo was in there somewhere. I needed to find it.

When I arrived at the warehouse with eight or ten helpers, it was clear the task at hand amounted to a very small needle in several hundred haystacks; there were hundreds of filing cabinets, each bulging with contracts, memos, letters, message slips, and every other conceivable variety of paper that would have been generated by such an operation over a twelve-year span in, ironically, the precomputer age. I instructed our small army to closely examine every page, in every drawer, in every file cabinet, giving them a week to complete the task.

After a week . . . nothing. They'd gone through everything, I was told, and came up empty.

I flew to Oakland and met the team at the warehouse.

"*Everything*? Every drawer? Every piece of paper?"

"Yes."

"Are you positive?" I asked, randomly opening a filing cabinet. "Every last piece?"

The drawer I happened to open was full of invoices. They were on yellow onionskin paper, thinner than toilet tissue. There were hundreds if not thousands of them jammed into the file drawer. "Even these?"

"Well no," someone admitted, "why would we look at invoices?"

"Okay, look, apparently I didn't make myself clear. *Every* piece, no matter its purpose, no matter what color."

Three days later, I get a call. They'd found it—apparently accidentally stapled to the back of one of those yellow invoices. We had worked hard to get that lucky!

The case went to trial in Judge McCullum's Alameda County courtroom in September 1986. The jury came back with their verdict on the day before Thanksgiving. In between, there was plenty of drama.

Since the rules of evidence at the time allowed you to impeach a witness with new documents if you could show he lied on the stand, I keep the damning Bowman document carefully under wraps. So, when it's my turn to cross-examine Bowman, after the other side has had him repeat his bogus story, I walk behind him, reach over his shoulder, and lay the memo in front of him, simultaneously introducing it as a new exhibit. For a long moment he stares at it, the thing's *in his own handwriting*, and goes white.

The other side's going ape, wildly objecting, but the judge—who was also the judge in the first trial—cuts them off with a sharp: "I don't think so, this is clearly impeachment."

Of course, we end up blowing them out of the water. A book written about the two trials would be entitled *Once Upon a Time in ComputerLand*. What made the situation so unusual, and indeed unprecedented, was that in two cases, both with identical facts tried before the same judge, the first ended in a verdict against defendant Millard for a California record in punitive damages, while the second was a complete defense victory, the plaintiffs receiving zero and Millard getting total vindication.

I took a picture of the Bowman memo, framed it, and put it on my desk—right next to my million-dollar bonus check. But I now had to deal with the big verdict from the first Millard case, which was on appeal and still threatening the future of the company.

Hafif had won the first trial, I won the second one, so we decide to meet in his office to see if we could reach some sort of meeting of the minds. The fact is, if we can't, it's a lose-lose. If Hafif doesn't back off, ComputerLand is facing bankruptcy due to the punitive damages.

His office is immense, reflecting his ego, and from the outset, it's clear the negotiation won't be easy. Hafif detests Millard even more than I realized; it's personal with him, he's loaded for bear, civilian casualties be damned.

"Listen," he says, "you seem to be an okay guy, but your client is the biggest asshole in the world, and I'm gonna take him apart!"

"Whoa, whoa, whoa!" I reply, raising both hands in surrender. "I feel the same way about your clients, but that won't help us resolve this thing." I pause. "And I gotta tell you, Herb, I'm kind've surprised to see this side of you."

Pulling back my lapel, I reveal a HERB HAFIF FOR GOVERNOR pin, scrounged for the purpose from one of his supporters, "because I voted for you for governor."

Honest to God, it was like all the venom just went out of him. He looked at me for what felt like half a minute, then smiled. "Okay, what is it you want?"

It was a phenomenon I've experienced more than once in complicated negotiations, before and since: How, when you turn an adversarial situation into a human one, the walls can come tumbling down.

By the time we left that room, we'd struck a deal. With his support, I'd go out and try to sell the company. If our side won the appeal, which seemed likely, they'd still end up with 12 percent of the company; and if they won, they'd get 20 percent. Either way, the 45 percent goes away, and so do the punitive damages.

And, by the way, once I get to know him, Herb Hafif is actually a terrific guy and one heck of a lawyer. He understood that the punitives would bankrupt the company, voiding all the franchise agreements, meaning his clients could end up with nothing. On the other hand, if they let the punitives go and kept the 45 percent, they had 45 percent of a private company where Millard still held 55 percent. Again, they could be left out in the cold. The only chance for a payday for Herb and his clients was to sell the company—and I was the only one who could convince William to do that.

Of course, now I have to go out and sell the company, and it soon narrows down to three potential buyers—Warburg, Pincus in New York; the Pritzkers in Chicago; and Bell Canada, headquartered in Toronto. For several months, I pinball between those three cities. trying to work the number up, before we finally settled on Warburg, Pincus.

And that seems to be that. Unlikely as it seemed as first, that call for a courtesy meeting with Millard has had a huge payoff. Not only has it gotten me back into law—civil this time, and at the very highest level—but it created relationships with William and a host of others that would lead to all kinds of other possibilities.

The same strategies, attention to detail, and techniques that worked well in criminal defense had transitioned beautifully to civil trials. I kept the team together, and over the twenty-one years since, I've gone on to try fifty-nine more civil cases, always for causes and clients I believed in. Some of my closest friends today I met first as clients. (One of my favorites was Ron Waranch, a very successful builder in Southern California and a fellow member of Horatio Alger. Ron's daughter, Sally, worked for me as an office manager and recommended me to her father. Seven trials, seven victories. Before Ron passed away in 2010, he asked me to be trustee of his estate for the benefit of his daughters, including Sally. It has been a wonderful relationship that has gone full circle.)

In short, the ComputerLand case produced the three commodities I'm always after in my professional life: fun, profit, and friendship. But what I don't know yet is that there's still some serious drama to come.

Since the ComputerLand sale is a cash deal, with heavy tax implications, Millard has decided to move his entire family to Saipan, in the Northern Marianas, where the effective tax rate for residents is only 5 percent. No problem there, all perfectly legal—until the *Wall Street Journal* gets hold of the story that William Millard's relocated to the other side of the world to avoid taxes, a gigantic red flag in the face of the IRS bull if ever there was one. Soon the House Ways and Means Committee (under chairman and future federal inmate Dan Rostenkowski, D-Chicago) gets in on the act, promulgating a new regulation that *retroactively* changes the rules, imposing major tax liabilities on William by passing what they referred to as "the Millard amendment."

Since I've been flying over to Saipan every six weeks anyway, now that he's at war with the Feds, I take that on, too. The result? Fortunately, their ability to write new law was as sloppy as their integrity! I win the tax case for William.

Then one day, I get a call from my receptionist, in tears—there are four IRS agents in our office. In the sweepstakes for the two things you never want to hear, this runs a close second to: "*Sixty Minutes* is in the office."

Just so there's no doubt as to why they're targeting me, all four are holding copies of the newly published book about the Millard case (*Once Upon a Time in ComputerLand*) and my role in it.

The upshot is, unable to get Millard, they've invented all kinds of income for me I never made, which has me owing ten million dollars in taxes and penalties. Fighting it would be an incredibly stressful ordeal that would go on for quite a while.

Yet ghastly as it was, even this was a kind of opportunity. For it led me to Dave Dalton.

Dave's the most brilliant mind on taxation out there, a decorated ex-marine jet pilot whom Fortune 500 corporations keep on a $400,000 retainer just to be available. He, too, would become a lifelong friend. And, by the way, he not only resolved my tax audit, but got me a refund. The guy is truly amazing!

Dave has been my wingman on multiple deals ever since. Not only has he become my closest friend, he's been the very embodiment of the maxim that "in business, never choose yourself—you've already got one of those."

Temperamentally, the two of us are mirror images, complementing each another perfectly. For all his success, Dave may be the most compulsively cynical and pessimistic individual on the face of the Earth. And I'm just as compulsively optimistic, imbued with this sense that anything can be made to happen by sheer force of will. So, over the years, Dave has been my due diligence in the flesh. If Dave Dalton, as my partner, signs off on a business venture, I *know* it's a go.

When word of the role I'd played in the Millard/ComputerLand saga got around, it launched my ancillary career as a freelance troubleshooter, someone who could be counted on to step into a complicated situation and find the win-win.

Not that it was a role with which I was completely unfamiliar. Years before, Richard Pryor had come to me needing someone with both criminal experience (criminal, because at the time he was facing charges, having just almost burned himself alive freebasing) and civil, since he was suing everyone from his agent in Atlanta to the *National Enquirer*. Privately very quiet, polite, and almost painfully shy, Richard was the opposite of the guy onstage, and it was clear why he might have used drugs and alcohol—because when he was sober, he wasn't Richard Pryor. Sober, he wouldn't even use a four-letter word.

While I was advising Richard, his Hollywood super-agent, Skip Brittenham, negotiated a record five-picture deal with Columbia worth $40 million. The first of them, *Richard Pryor—Live on the Sunset Strip*, created an entire new genre of great stand-up comedy performances turned into major concert films. As I was sitting beside him at the premiere, when he was still more client than friend, he at one point leaned over, squeezed my arm, and whispered, "You'll like this part."

"Lawyers, you know how expensive they are?" he asked on-screen a moment later. "I got this one lawyer—I just met the motherfucker, and he charged me $30,000."

That was me! I whispered back, "Hey, that was just the retainer."

In December 1982, I received a call from the White House. President Reagan had been taking some heat for not doing enough for black causes. He decided to push forward an agenda item to make Martin Luther King Jr.'s birthday a national holiday. Armstrong Williams, a legislative analyst at the Department of Agriculture who had previously interned for South Carolina Republican Senator Strom Thurmond, was given the job of pulling together an event on Martin Luther King Jr.'s birthday in Washington, D.C., in January 1983. Armstrong decided to go for the brass ring and try to get Richard Pryor to headline the event.

For us, the timing was ideal, since we were looking for positive press to offset the negatives surrounding the notorious drug and fire incident. But far from a mere public relations coup, the event was enormously meaningful to Richard, and it produced one of the greatest performances of his brilliant life. On the plane to D.C., Richard shared some of his speech, and he started to tear up. It was riveting, and I knew right then he would be a smash hit. His address in front of a thousand people at the Department of Agriculture was the best speech I have ever heard. He broke down in tears three times, captured the essence of Martin Luther King Jr.'s civil rights crusade, and the next morning the headline in the *Washington Post* was "The Jester Weeps." From that moment on, the national holiday celebrating Martin Luther King Jr.'s birthday was a lock. I always thought it might have been one of the most important performances of Richard's talented life. It was straight from his heart, and, in my view, he never got enough recognition for the critical role he played.

Still, Richard had basically been a one-off. Thanks to the Millard experience, troubleshooting now became a key part of my professional portfolio. Indeed, among the most appealing aspects of these special projects is their sheer variety. Everyone is a unique experience, featuring people I'd never encounter in conventional business settings.

Take, for instance, Andy Bleiler.

All-but-forgotten now, for a few days in January 1998 he was the focus of nationwide attention. The Monica Lewinsky scandal was just exploding when, as the *Washington Post*'s provocative headline told it: "Lewinsky's Former Teacher Discloses Affair."

That would be Andy.

He'd been Monica's drama teacher at Portland State when they began a relationship that, as the story reported, "continued until last year, throughout much of the time she reportedly has alleged she had an intimate relationship with President Clinton."

I got involved via a great public relations guy I knew, Mike Nason, whose niece happened to be Bleiler's wife, who herself had only recently learned of her husband's infidelity. Mike tells me all hell is breaking loose in Portland, and, not even stopping to pack a bag, I catch the first flight up there. Sure enough, I find media camped out on the Bleilers' patch of front lawn, baying for red meat. In my suit and tie, I must look like I'm in the know, because they're instantly on me like ravenous dogs.

The Bleilers are barricaded inside this little house, along with a few friends and neighbors, and since they've hammered blankets over the windows to block out the flood-lights, it looks like a scene from *Apocalypse Now*. When I ask if there's any place we can talk privately, they lead me up to this tiny attic space, where it's hotter than hell, and start telling their story.

Up to now, I've assumed my job will be to defend Bleiler from the charge of sex with a minor. But, no, that isn't it; in fact, she was eighteen at the time.

It's much bigger than that. They tell me that ever since Monica got to the White House, she's been writing them regularly—and, basically to impress them with her proximity to power, she's been forwarding material from Clinton's desk.

"Really?"

"Would you like to see it?"

Heck, yeah!

It's less a treasure trove of state secrets than random reports and documents she thought would give them a cheap thrill. A memorandum might include a mention of the name "Andy," or the name similar to the name of their street, and these she'd have highlighted. But there was no question it all came from the White House.

At this point, Monica's been in the public eye just a couple of days, and I start asking the obvious questions: What kind of person is she behind closed doors? Do they believe the reports about her relationship with Clinton? Because the president is denying everything—and so, for the moment, is she.

Well, says Andy, before leaving for her internship at the White House, she did say she she'd be sure to earn her "presidential kneepads." They also tell me she's told them about a three-way involving Clinton, Monica, and a cigar.

A little while later, I go outside to address the press. I tell them we do not have definitive information on whether Monica Lewinsky had an affair with President Clinton. But what we can say is that she's no shrinking violet—and, throwing out a king-sized bone, I offer up the kneepads line.

Which, of course, sets them off, shouting and clamoring for more, but I hold up my hands and add that whatever else I have, I'll be dispensing at a hotel in downtown Portland. "Now, we'd appreciate it if everyone got off these people's lawn, so that they can take their kids to school."

Since Ken Starr's investigators, whom I already have contacted, won't be getting there until Monday, I have to spend the rest of the week in a Portland hotel, and the entire media scrum follows me there. The hotel's management is so delighted they end up buying me the clothes and sundries I neglected to bring with me. When I get to my room there are, no exaggeration, sixty-five interview requests from the national media. That Sunday morning, I appear on all the morning news shows.

It was not very long afterward that Monica finally admitted to the affair and turned over her own evidence to Starr's team—the blue dress with the presidential stain. While I have no way to prove it, my guess was that she only fessed up and cut a deal to avoid prosecution after being confronted with the evidence Andy gave them: the material she sent to Andy from the White House.

That part of the story was never reported.

Most of these special projects are short-term. I get paid a one-time fee, go to work, and in six months or less, if the problems are solvable, I'll usually have them solved; there's little need for assistants, researchers, or associates. It's just me, flying solo.

A typical case was one of the wealthiest men in Indonesia, who was desperate to get into the United States to see his son graduate from Harvard but couldn't get a visa after being convicted of illegal campaign contributions to (guess who!) the Clintons. That was not an easy one, since Mrs. Clinton was secretary of state at the time. But we got it done.

Then there was the English gentleman I represented who was once the best backgammon player in the world. He'd come under investigation because in the course of looking into Kirk Kerkorian's application for a gambling license, it was discovered that my guy had won more than $100 million over an eight-year period from Kerkorian through sports betting. The authorities were concerned my client was a bookie (he wasn't) because that would have created major issues for Kirk—who was the majority holder of MGM Grand and all of their casinos.

Maybe it's my OCD, but I just can't stand leaving loose ends in anything I do. That's why, gratifying as were the ComputerLand court victory and the successful sale of the company that followed, there remained one last bit of business that preyed on my mind—and William Millard's. He was royally upset about the million dollars he'd paid out in 1985 for the half-assed, ineffectual defense in the first trial, and he was absolutely right to be.

Though it was a lawyer in Edward Bennett Williams's firm who'd done such a lousy job, that didn't make me think any less of Mr. Williams himself. Not only had I long considered him the best lawyer America has ever produced, I also admired how he'd managed to achieve equal success as an entrepreneur. As a sports fan, I was especially impressed by his ownership of, first, the Washington Redskins, and, then, the Baltimore Orioles.

So, it was kind of strange, now that I was arranging to finally meet my hero, that it was to ask him to refund a million dollars in fees for mistakes his firm made in the first ComputerLand trial.

I decide the best approach is to count on Ed Williams's character, so when we meet at his Washington office, I open with a frank declaration of admiration. "The truth is, if you told me the sky was black, Mr. Williams, I'd believe it—that's how much respect I have for you. And while I know you don't have the time to read the entire trial transcript, if you'll read the crucial twenty pages I'll leave with you, and you tell me that what you see there is good lawyering, then I'll assume everything I believe is dead wrong, and tell Mr. Millard it *was* good lawyering, because Edward Bennett Williams said so. If, on the other hand, you agree this is some of the worst lawyering you have ever seen in your long and storied legal career, I hope you'll do the right thing and give Mr. Millard back his million dollars."

I knew the twenty pages would take about eighteen minutes to read. It was Herb Hafif's speech to Mr. Millard after he called him to the stand in the first trial. I say a speech, because for eighteen minutes Herb, in front of the jury, told William what a bastard and a liar he was and how he was going to prove it. No questions! Just editorial. Millard's lawyer just sat there. No objection. Nothing! Probably the worst example of lawyering I have ever seen—or even heard of.

Ed Williams politely listened to my spiel and said, "Well, I'm not going to commit to anything, but why don't you leave that twenty pages with me?" With that, we shook hands, and I left.

A few weeks later, he calls and asks me to meet him at his place in New York City. So I fly to New York, and go up to his apartment, and soon we repair to his favorite watering hole down the block. We're both Scotch drinkers, and before long, he gets expansive, telling one wonderful court story after another. We end up sitting there for a good five hours, no dinner, just drinking and shooting the breeze, and by the end, I like and admire him even more than I did before.

It's then that he tells me he has cancer. He's been fighting it for more than ten years but is starting to feel like he's losing the battle. It's quite an admission, and it's impossible not to feel for this incredible man.

Yet through it all, he's never once raised the subject of Millard and the million dollars, and I'm certainly not about to raise it. In a touchy negotiation, it's pretty close to axiomatic that the first one to raise the forbidden subject loses.

We finally stagger back to his place, say goodnight, and he disappears into the lobby and goes up. I stumble back to my hotel, and the next day I fly home with the mother of all hangovers.

Another three or four weeks go by before I hear from Ed again. Marvin Davis, who is represented by Ed Williams, is selling the Beverly Hills Hotel to the Sultan of Brunei, and Ed is setting up an office at the hotel to complete this transaction. He asks me to come up and see him. This time, there's no goofing around. As soon as I arrive, he gets right to Millard.

"You really want me to refund that million dollars?" he demands.

"Yes sir, I do."

"Do you realize how much money that is?"

"Well, I don't know, but reading the papers, I notice it's a lot less than you're paying your star player on the Orioles, Eddie Murray, who is currently hitting a buck twenty-five."

At this, Williams pauses, then bursts out laughing. "Okay, Terry"—by now we're on a first-name basis—"look, I've never refunded a fee in my life, but this time I am going to. You want to know why?"

"Why?"

"Because I'm probably not going to beat this latest bout of cancer. I think I'm going to die. And when I do, the last thing I want is a son of a bitch like you suing my widow!"

He laughed, and I hoped he was joking. Until that moment, I did not know it was possible for me to have even greater respect for this giant in the legal arena. His integrity and professionalism were second to none.

Several months after the meeting at the Beverly Hills Hotel, Edward Bennett Williams, the greatest lawyer who ever lived, passed away.

Even now, reflecting back on it, I'm staggered by the range of experiences and opportunities that unfolded in my life because of agreeing to that first lunch with William Millard. A "nothing" lunch had materialized into several adventures of a lifetime.

CHAPTER TEN

Good Vibrations— Great Results

Integrity breeds success

I suppose it was no accident that it was at this point in my life that I got involved in the battle against the Catholic Church on behalf of the priest victims.

Years before, when I'd moved on to my new career as an entrepreneur and businessman, I'd been bound and determined to do only good in the world and have tried hard to fulfill that vow. As a car salesman, I certainly wanted to make money, but I also had to have a great product, and then sell it at the fairest price, and stand foursquare behind our warranties. Again, as a banker, and in multiple other arenas, I wanted to make money, but never at the price of not operating with absolute integrity.

What's telling is how much such a commitment contributed to my success. Why? Because in business there is nothing so precious as a reputation for honesty and integrity. I get opportunities all the time because somebody, often a stranger, has heard something good about me. And sometimes these strangers become not just associates, but the closest of friends.

Once the Millard case brought me back to the law on the civil side, in fifty-nine more civil trials I'd found numerous opportunities to do good in that realm, as well. And now, representing the victims of child sexual abuse was the culmination of all that.

Nor was it a coincidence that it came my way via a young woman named Kathy Freberg. Or that Kathy is a fellow graduate of Pepperdine School of Law.

I run into people all the time who make a point in the first five minutes of telling you that they went to law school at Harvard, or Yale, or Stanford. I'm always equally delighted to tell them where I went: Pepperdine.

More than forty years later, I look back on that decision as one of the smartest and luckiest I ever made. Had I gone anywhere else, I might still have the career success I enjoy today, but I'd surely not be as successful a human being. I left Pepperdine with not only an excellent grounding in the law, but also with the powerful understanding of how it should be properly used, and, when it is necessary (as in my case it was), having the internal capacity to make a midcourse correction.

I recently caught a terrific documentary about the late-1980s rivalry between college football powerhouses Notre Dame and the University of Miami called *Catholics Versus Convicts*. It features a guy named Pat Walsh. Smart and aggressively entrepreneurial—definitely a member of the 15 percent—his lifelong obsession was to play basketball for the Irish, and he'd just been accepted, as a walk-on, when at the last minute the dream was snatched away. He'd defied an administrative edict forbidding the creation of T-shirts without the school's sanction; and though he pleaded, *begged*, for another chance, he never got one.

It is easy to take it as a sad story—for all the successes he's racked up ever since, he's never gotten over that disappointment. "It's a constant reminder for me," he says toward the documentary's close, "that you gotta do things the right way."

But what he doesn't say, and doesn't have to, is that if he was unlucky enough to attend a school where the commitment to honesty and fair dealing was absolute, in the end he was also fortunate. Cruel as the lesson was, he's profited by it ever since.

I totally identify.

There's an ongoing philosophic debate, going back to the Greeks, on whether ethical behavior is second nature or innate. But there is little question that in the face of the modern world's never-ending temptations, it needs a lot of reinforcement. Not so long ago, society itself was set up to provide just that, starting with stable families, religious institutions, and even an entertainment culture that saw instruction by heroic example as part of its mission. Yet if those institutions have all been in sharp decline, arguably none has taken a harder hit in this regard than the educational establishment. At many of our schools and universities the very notion of pushing anything resembling traditional moral standards is regarded with frank outrage and horror.

Not at Pepperdine.

Let's put it this way: In an era where it's hard to open a paper or click onto a news website without finding another story about bribery, corruption, or official malfeasance, I've personally never run across a single one about a Pepperdine grad.

Founded in 1970, the law school had just opened when I got there—I was part of its first full-time graduating class in 1974—but already its stress on ethics and values was paramount. Although a Christian school, it is entirely ecumenical in approach; other religious traditions are held in great respect, and their precepts taught. There are something like forty-two different religious clubs on campus.

While many schools offer courses in morality and ethics, in no other are they so explicitly promoted throughout the curriculum, brought to bear in every class, and every subject. The conscious objective is to turn out not just quality students and lawyers, but quality human beings.

First as a student at the law school, later as an adjunct professor, and for the last twenty-five years as a member of the Board of Regents, over and over I've seen up close and personal how the school's leaders have lived out the school's creed. Ron Phillips, who still holds the record as the longest-tenured dean at any law school in the country and now Pepperdine's vice chancellor, may be the most generous and open-spirited person I have ever met; and Andy Benton, the president and CEO for nineteen years, is his closest challenger. Andy's home and office were constantly buzzing with student visitors, and it is understood that no subject or point of view is ever off the table or out of bounds. Faith-based positive thinking and Current Best Ideas are alive and well at Pepperdine. In this way and a hundred others, the entire administration and professors set an extraordinarily high bar for us graduates to live up to in our own professional and personal lives.

It is not always easy. After all, I emerged from the place as a lawyer, a profession in which compromise (moral and otherwise) is often the name of the game. For many in the field, finding ways to live with oneself becomes a second job.

I take particular satisfaction in the fact that it was a Pepperdine alum, Kathy Freberg, who drew me into the lawsuit against the Catholic Church on behalf of the priest victims.

Even by Pepperdine standards, Kathy had already proven herself a special breed of lawyer, as principled and tenacious as they come. She first came to my attention as a student, when she won the annual law school scholarship in my name awarded to the third-year class's MVP, and I subsequently recruited her to join me as cocounsel representing UNLV basketball coach Jerry Tarkanian in his landmark suit against the NCAA. A basketball player herself, and a huge fan of Tark's, Kathy shared the future College Hall of Fame coach's fully justified outrage at being singled out for alleged recruiting violations. She worked like hell to make them squirm, in ways that bullies far too seldom do. Days before we were to go to trial, the NCAA caved, settling for $2.5 million, the first time they were ever forced to admit defeat, giving Tark both total vindication and a pretty good payday in an age when even great coaches were making $300,000 a year.

Kathy had been off on her own for a while, going great guns, when I hear from her. She tells me she has a client who went to Mater Dei High, the premier Catholic high school in Southern California, who claims that as a student he was molested by the school's principal. Apparently one of my former partners in my old firm is representing the Catholic Church in Orange County, and Kathy asks if I'll contact him to see if a settlement can be reached.

When I meet my friend, I'm pretty sure in advance what the answer will be, since the priest scandal has not yet exploded nationwide, and the Church's stance is to deny everything. I tell him that Kathy is prepared to settle the case for a million dollars, and there's a pause, followed almost immediately by a bemused chuckle, and the words: "No way."

Three years later they end up having to settle for $5.2 million.

How did it happen? While I soon joined her in litigating the case, most of the credit goes to Kathy, who, with her usual zeal, dug in places no one ever looked before and found mountains of dirt, starting with the existence of a Church hospital in New Mexico set up to treat pedophiles. It turns out that our priest underwent treatment there just before being assigned to an all-boys' school—Mater Dei High School in Orange County, California.

A year later, when the California State Legislature extended the statute of limitations, Kathy and I teamed up with a third lawyer, Steve Rubino—a legend who'd been fighting the Church way back when nobody believed the truth—to handle 150 of California's eight hundred cases. I was the lead trial lawyer. Steve, a great trial lawyer in his own right, was the resident expert on the Catholic Church and the best negotiator I ever saw. Kathy, with her command of the endless documents involved in the case, was our legal wizard and motions guru. She was also the "heart" of our team and had endless calming conversations with our clients and their families.

In LA County, the plaintiffs got to pick the first case to go to trial, so naturally we chose the most gruesome, nine victims of the same priest. The details were so stomach-turning that the Church settled all the cases before this first one even went to trial. The priest ended up fleeing to Mexico, and when the police located him there, he jumped off a rooftop before they could arrest him. That, at least, is the official version. There's also an unofficial version.

But in San Diego County, the Church got to select the first case, and they chose another of our cases, one that looked to be a likely winner for them. This victim was a rare female who, at the time of her molestation, had been seventeen years old, not eight or nine, so it could be portrayed as a consensual encounter, though the priest was denying there'd been any physical contact at all. The Church figured they could settle this case at a very low number, setting a precedent for the ones to follow. After all, the San Diego priest records had all been destroyed in what they euphemistically called a "routine bureaucratic housecleaning."

It was classic Church arrogance—they'd gotten away with dissembling so often, for so long, they thought themselves invulnerable.

Until, that is, Steve unearthed a *copy* of the priest's supposedly incinerated file in an archive in San Bernardino. It contained a document wherein the priest in question admitted outright that he'd raped our client multiple times.

We produced this information three days before we were to pick the jury, and the San Diego diocese immediately filed for bankruptcy to stop us from proceeding and releasing the information to the public. At every bankruptcy hearing that followed, we urged the federal judge, one of several spectacular judges we dealt with on these cases, to simply threaten to release the case, knowing they would settle rather than let the facts be known to the world. Finally, she did exactly that, and, abracadabra—that's what happened.

Steve and I would subsequently work together again on another high-profile case, though one where the tragedy was limited to a single illustrious family—the heirs of Dr. Martin Luther King Jr.

I'd met Dr. King's widow, Coretta, long before, through Richard Pryor's involvement on behalf of the Martin Luther King Jr. holiday, and Coretta invited me down to Ebenezer Baptist Church in Atlanta for Easter services in 1984. At the time, the patriarch, Martin Luther King Sr., was still alive, and I'll never forget sitting beside him at Easter dinner as he described the Sunday morning a gunman burst into Ebenezer Baptist Church in the middle of his sermon and started shooting up the place, killing his wife at the organ. The pain of that loss, so soon after losing his son, must have been unbearable.

After Coretta died, this connection led indirectly to my getting involved in the long-running dispute among the King children over the King estate. The genesis of the problem was that the oldest sister, Yolanda, who was supposed to take charge after her mother passed, died unexpectedly soon after, leaving the three younger siblings to fend for themselves. They barely knew their father and had no real experience in handling business.

I had real empathy for them. As I'd seen often in Hollywood, even under the best of circumstances, the children of exceptionally important and powerful people tend to have a problem forging their own identity. But what do you do when your father is a saint, his birthday a national holiday? How do you even make a living? It's not like, if you're Martin Luther King Jr.'s kid, you can easily escape the expectations of the public at large.

Easy as it was for outsiders to condemn, it was hard to blame them for seeming to cash in on their name as the obvious way to go—especially since their father had trademarked his vast trove of historic material and left it not to any museum, but to the family.

By the time I got involved, they were at one another's throats. Some of Dr. King's papers had been sold, but there were ongoing fights over how the money should be divided, two of the three had filed suit against the other, and that was just the start of the bad blood.

In 2010, I was appointed as trustee of the King Estate by Superior Court Judge Ural Granville, granted power to make decisions the siblings couldn't make for themselves, and I brought in Steve Rubino to help me. For the next two and a half years, we worked closely with Judge Granville, whose temperament and aptitude made him one of the best judges I have had the pleasure to work with. During that time, there was relative peace within the family. When we took it over, the estate was about $2 million in debt; by the time we left, the debt had been settled, they had over a million dollars in the bank, and the estate was producing about $700,000 in annual income.

Yet almost as soon as we extricated ourselves, they were at war again, with one actually wanting to sell off their father's Nobel Peace Prize and personal bible, the one Barack Obama used when he took the oath of office.

While it was a sad and difficult situation on multiple levels, all three siblings are good people and, at the core, well meaning. I hope they find peace.

As for Kathy, she wasn't yet finished with the Catholic hierarchy. Even with the settlement concluded, she wanted to get the internal church documents released and force the Church to confront publicly the evil that had been perpetrated. After two more years, she finally succeeded.

It's called integrity. And in business as in everyday life, there is no quality more vital—or, in myriad ways, more certain to create success. When you do right by people, the world pays you back in full, often many times over. I like to think Kathy and I have a lot in common, but the most important is that we both went to Pepperdine School of Law.

Pepperdine taught character, and character shows up in conduct.

CHAPTER ELEVEN

Mistakes Worth Making

You are never too big to fail—or to learn from failure

I'm sometimes asked, even by those who know me well, what I was thinking in the run-up to the 2016 presidential campaign. How in the world did I end up heading up the presidential campaign of Ben Carson?

Though it's a complicated question, the answer is really pretty straightforward—in fact, the one embedded in these pages. The decision was driven by my sense of how vital it is that others embrace the basic understandings that animate those who've achieved high levels of success—starting with the reality that the 15 percent is *not* an exclusionary club; with enough drive, guts, and perseverance, anyone can make it. Many of its members get in not despite, but *because* they grew up facing daunting obstacles, of necessity coming early to high levels of self-reliance and resilience.

But—need it be said?—for too many today the identical circumstances produce the opposite effect, giving rise to a

chip-on-the-shoulder worldview marked by perpetual petti-
ness and envy. Since the game is rigged, so this thinking goes,
why even bother to try? Indeed, why behave ethically when
looking out exclusively for "number one" is the way to get
ahead? Alas, nowhere is this mentality more evident than in
America's courthouses, where the docket is clogged with lawsuits—and even criminal complaints!—that put corner cutting, petty resentments, and outright greed on full display.

I once represented Robert Schuller, the internationally
renowned architect of the Crystal Cathedral and *Hour of
Power*, in one of the most mind-bogglingly pointless cases on
record. Bob was en route from California to New York to pre-
side over the funeral of Betty Shabazz, Malcolm X's widow,
and asked a male flight attendant if he would hang his robes
so they wouldn't wrinkle. Nice a guy as Bob was, his evange-
lism (or his celebrity) rubbed some people the wrong way, and
the flight attendant was apparently one of those. He not only
refused Bob's request, but pointedly stuffed the garment into
an overhead bin. There followed a heated exchange, during
which the flight attendant maintained that the cleric attacked
him. It probably bears mentioning that the male flight attendant was twenty-nine and Schuller seventy-five. Nonetheless,
sensitivities about air travel being what they are, the FBI was
waiting to arrest Bob when the plane landed in New York.
Easiest case I ever had dismissed—along with the civil suit the
flight attendant later filed. The attendant's flight of fantasy
was all about getting an unearned payday.

We are of course fortunate that religion doesn't divide
us in this country to the degree it sometimes has elsewhere.
One of my grandmothers was Southern Baptist, so when I
stayed with her, I was baptized Southern Baptist; the other
was Catholic, so she baptized me Catholic; and, for the heck
of it, my mom baptized me Presbyterian. I suppose each was

convinced following her way would get me to heaven, but in the end, no harm, no foul.

Still, we are increasingly divided these days by other kinds of tribalism, those that define us by class, social standing, ethnicity, or gender—and those encumbered by such thinking also live in victimhood, believing life is forever stacked against them by virtue of the circumstances, even the very bodies into which they were born. By definition, they see every difficult situation as hopeless and every obstacle insurmountable.

This is the tragic delusion of our age. The notion that we are unable to create our own lives and futures is a recipe not just for personal failure, but ultimately for societal and economic disaster. And it strikes me that those in the 15 percent have an even greater responsibility than others to address that delusion and point the way to others.

Enter Ben Carson.

If ever there existed anyone who could dispel the ugly message of giving up on life—that the race is fixed, so no point in even making it to the starting blocks—Ben is it. Celebrated as an extraordinarily accomplished pediatric surgeon, he rose from poverty to the highest reaches of American life solely by his own talent, drive, and self-belief.

Having come to know Ben through the Horatio Alger Association, I genuinely liked him. His grace and modesty were not for show, but absolutely real. The guy seemed a walking antidote to the poisonous victim mentality.

So in early 2015, when Ben and his adviser Armstrong Williams (by now a close friend whom I'd first met way back when I visited Washington with Richard Pryor) asked if I'd chair Ben's campaign. I thought it over and agreed.

However, my agreement came with the proviso that as we went about building the team, hiring consultants. gaining ballot access, and the rest, I'd be able to put in place a team of trusted nonpoliticos to keep an eye on the pros, making sure they didn't do what they famously do best: backstab, undercut one another, and use the campaign as a personal piggy bank.

The Sophie's Choice of politics was that you needed the professional politicos, because they had the contacts to set up the campaign structure nationwide and deal with the complications of ballot access, which was no easy task. I had set up Iowa and South Carolina (two of the first three primary contests) myself, but it was a tough job. I simply was unable, time-wise, to set up all fifty states, D.C., and assorted territories. We needed the politicos. But they also brought with them every bad character trait imaginable. The solution was to simultaneously build into the team people I could trust, who would be the watchdogs over the politicos. I hoped to get the best parts of the politicos and protect against their darker side.

The other challenge we faced was that lifelong politicians had a big advantage over the nonpoliticians regarding campaign and election laws. The professional politicians already had not just campaign staffs, but established Super PACs to support their candidacies. It is just a fact that unless you are a billionaire, you need both to be viable. But the real rub is that the campaign laws dictate that if you are involved in a Super PAC you have to be out of the day-to-day campaign for a minimum of 120 days. You cannot legally do both at the same time so are forced to decide which side of the line you are on. The goal for me became to (1) set up the campaign; (2) get the money machine rolling; (3) then, when Ben announced his candidacy in late May 2015, move over to the Super PAC and organize it; then (4) jump back into the campaign 120 days later by mid-October 2015. Meanwhile, I left meticulous plans for the 120-day interim. Extensive policy books were prepared for the debates and speeches, along with instructions that Ben begin giving major policy speeches in July and August. I expected that by building detailed, intelligent policy positions on a range of issues into his campaign rhetoric they would become second nature and pop out like toast when he was asked tough questions in the debates or if, God forbid, there was some type of national or world event he would have to address.

In the beginning, things seemed promising. As we had hoped, when Ben announced that spring, his nonestablishment candidacy set off a wave of grassroots enthusiasm, and with it came a massive influx of cash into his campaign coffers.

However, things started going bad when I left the formal campaign to organize Ben's super PAC. When I was gone, the politicos quickly got rid of the watchdogs, brought in their own people, and started spending like drunken sailors. As an example, of the $68 million raised between May and December 2015, only $2.5 million remained by the first primary contest—the Iowa caucus on February 1, 2016.

Speaking of Iowa, I had hired a terrific young man by the name of Ryan Rhodes to marshal and manage the Iowa caucuses. After the election I visited with Ryan about what went wrong in Iowa. I asked him specifically if interference by the Ted Cruz campaign (as was reported at the time) was at fault for Ben's poor showing. The answer was an emphatic "no," but what he then told me was distressing. He explained that the campaign headquarters in Virginia refused to give him the tools he needed to win. For instance, he had asked for thousands of bumper stickers in the run-up to the caucuses. The campaign paid top dollar and shipped Ryan bumper stickers made out of paper. Paper?! In Iowa?! The first rain and the stickers dissolved from the bumpers. The real issue? Who made them and how much of a kickback did the politicos receive?

Additionally, Ryan, in the last ninety days before the caucuses, begged for Carson yard signs—but very few materialized. After the campaign cratered within weeks of the Iowa caucuses, Ryan was asked to go up north and clean out a warehouse he had not known existed that supposedly held Carson campaign materials. First, the warehouse was owned by a brother of one of the politicos. Second, inside were 55,000 boxes of unused yard signs.

Why, you might ask, would anyone withhold yard signs from the campaign? The politicos had set up a website where they were selling yard signs. Overpay and get a kickback from the manufacturer; then refuse to give the materials to the campaign so the politicos can instead sell them on a website and pocket the money: these are just a sampling of how you turn $68 million into $2.5 million before the first primary.

Aside from the numerals in the bank accounts of the politicos and their buddies, there was nothing to show for all that money raised.

While it was no surprise that Ben had an unusually calm and relaxed manner, I'd seen that, or chosen to see it, as a strength, as it had been in his life as a surgeon. But what I began to understand now was that he seemed averse to conflict. While I was barred from speaking to people in the campaign by federal law for 120 days while organizing the Super PAC, I could still talk to the candidate, and as I watched with horror the unraveling of what I had envisioned and put together, I pleaded over and over with Ben to please stand up to the politicos. I just got silence. Nothing happened, except maybe the cash got drained even faster.

My opinion is that Ben fell victim to what psychologist Tim Levine refers to as the "Theory of Truth Default." If you have lived a life where detecting lies is not a skill set, it is human to assume truth, even in the face of overwhelming evidence. It is this human condition that allows fraud to work—over and over again.

Also, Ben's lack of command of the issues was becoming all too clear to the voting public. Brilliant as he was in his own field, I took it for granted he would bury himself in the policy papers and issue books we'd prepared and quickly get up to speed. To the contrary, the politicos who were now running his campaign were far too happy to have Ben singing the same tune that he had done for years—his stirring life story—while they gutted the campaign of cash. They told him he didn't have to study and that the public loved him just the way he was. What Ben never got was that the public was now fully aware of his life story. He needed to shift gears and transform his appearances into policy speeches telling America how he would lead and solve the problems the average citizen faced. Ben needed to transform from being a great surgeon to being presidential. But that never happened. As a result, when the going got rougher, and Ben was confronted with anything with a passing resemblance to tough questions, the gaffes started coming and never stopped.

I don't blame Ben; he was misled by the politicos. I even understand the motive of the politicos: it was all about lining their pockets. The people in the campaign I have a harder time understanding are the campaign folks who saw what was happening, knew it was wrong, and still said and did nothing. They know who they are, and they should be ashamed.

By the time I could come back to the campaign, Ben and I disagreed about a number of things, and I quit the campaign on October 25, 2015. It was less than three months before Iowa, and on that day, he was leading Trump in the polls, but the writing was already in bold letters on the wall. Not only would the campaign soon be broke, the candidate—duped by those around him—was woefully unprepared. The Ben Carson for president boom was DOA.

Might Ben have been president? Given subsequent events, there's no doubt in my mind it could have happened. Like Trump, he was not a part of the despised system; but with his more amiable demeanor, he might have emerged as a genuine outsider, but without the negatives.

As vital as anything else, Ben was a different kind of candidate, one who might have truly bridged the racial divide instead of being taken by many as seeking to exploit it; someone who, rather than wallowing in past injustices, celebrates a nation great enough to have moved so far beyond them.

Quite simply, *any* serious effort to heal our nation seemed worth the effort. And I don't think anyone who's seen where those bitter divisions can lead—whether in Bosnia, Iraq, Uganda, India, or any of a dozen of our own cities in the United States—will disagree.

It is, of course, human nature to gravitate toward those of shared background and experience, and, though it carries negative connotations, even the concept of tribalism is generally benign. I'm in a tribe called Pepperdine grads, and another called St. Louis Cardinals fans, and a third called the Horatio Alger Association.

Yet we're at a point where tribalism increasingly divides America in more dangerous ways, setting group against group, with millions convinced they are victims of the past, victimized in the present, and destined to be forever victims in the future. Their *consciousness* is of victimhood, their *conversation* is rooted in victimhood, their *conduct* is that of the victim. It is a mind-set that dictates they can never stand on their own feet, exercising the power of their best selves. Played out over months and years and decades, it will inevitably sap the morale of an entire nation.

Meanwhile, even as it proceeds, too many are intimidated and look the other way.

Ben Carson was never like that. For all that went wrong in the campaign, he understands full well it was not for nothing our Founders settled on *E pluribus unum*, "Out of many, one," as the nation's motto. He knows from his own life experience what far too many today have forgotten. We're already in a great tribe—it's called "Americans."

So while I certainly recognize getting involved in a presidential campaign and venturing so far from my realm of professional expertise may not have been the most brilliant move I ever made, I put it in the category of *a mistake that was worth making.*

CHAPTER TWELVE

Positive Thinking Works . . . but So Does Negative Thinking

The ability to shrug off setbacks and forge ahead will make or break you

There's a story I sometimes tell when someone makes the mistake of thinking I'm smart.

One day in the early 1980s, I get a call from Ron Helm, one of my best friends in Seattle, about an investment I've just got to get into. "It can't miss," he says, "it's going to be really big. A string of coffeehouses! And the hook is, they serve all sorts of flavored coffees. Instead of costing a quarter a cup, they'll charge something like $1.50."

You know where this is going.

So why did I dismiss Starbucks out of hand as one of the most idiotic notions I'd ever heard? Because as a child of the

1950s, to me a coffeehouse was where the beatnik Maynard G. Krebs spouted poetry and hung out on *The Dobie Gillis Show*.

Who in his right mind would pay a buck fifty for a cup of coffee when you could get one for a quarter?

Right, and who would want to carry a computer around in his hand when he's got a perfectly good one sitting on his desk?

So, yes, over the years, I've made more than a few miscalculations. And each time, I've gone back to the mental drawing board afterward to figure out why, and maybe beat myself up a little while I'm doing it. It is good to feel the pain of failure, as long as you learn the lessons and then move on. You can't get stuck wallowing in your mistakes. You can't let a negative result break your positive spirit.

Prepare for success, everyone says. But far more useful is preparing for failure, because that's where the great life lessons are found. Indeed, since failure can come in so many permutations, it's important to be a lifelong learner. The 15 percent excel in processing failure and moving past it. Why? Because most of them were born into and grew up surrounded by failure. For them failure is like water off a duck's back. As Mike Todd famously said, "Poor is a state of mind. Broke is a temporary condition."

Still, over the years, I've found a refresher course has sometimes been useful to reinforce the basics:

Arrogance is deadly: Start thinking you are bulletproof and get ready to take one in the heart.

Deal with disappointment but do not dwell on it: We are often defined by our ability to move on.

And above all:

Positivity works, but so does negativity: And it is the surest road to paralysis and failure.

Why is it that positive things tend to happen in the lives of positive people? I think it has to do with the messages we send out to the world. Whether we're aware of it or not, every one of us is a transmitter, the waves we're sending out received by anyone who happens to tune into our station, from business associates, to family, to the person behind the checkout counter at the supermarket. When we're thinking positive thoughts, it shows on our faces, in our voices, in the way we walk, in a hundred other ways.

And so does negativity.

In criminal law, I'd often use lie detectors, which, while not foolproof, are a terrific tool. Because unless you're a sociopath or have had CIA-level instruction in advanced lying, subtle changes in the body under questioning are unavoidable.

Think of the world as that machine, picking up those signals—and, as anyone in the 15 percent will tell you, it pays off emotionally, psychologically, and financially to transmit positivity and optimism.

How do we keep negativity at bay and make positivity a habit?

Start with perspective. The world is a big, complicated place, rife with wars, disease, and famine, which is to say, in the grand scheme of things, most of the setbacks and disappointments we experience in our lives (excepting those involving life and death) really aren't that big a deal. Of course, we all know this in theory, which is why it's so incredible how rarely we bring such an understanding to bear when it most obviously applies. Yes, that deal could have worked out better, but as a work experience it still beats the hell out of scavenging for rags in the slums of Mumbai.

How to foster optimism? When I speak to young people, they're often taken aback when I advise them to study quantum physics. But, in fact, the physical universe has real application to the challenges and possibilities in our own lives. For the closer we look, the more evident it becomes that nothing is impossible. Literally *nothing*. Albert Einstein, at the turn of the twentieth century, established the basis for two fundamental principles, general relativity and quantum theory. Later, geniuses like Richard Feynman, Roger Penrose, Jim Hartle, and Stephen Hawking have expanded on quantum mechanics to an extraordinary degree.

Staring at a wall, it seems utter lunacy to think, "I'm gonna move right through that thing." Yet, theoretically, that wall, made up as it is of molecules, atoms, and quarks, is *not* impenetrable; for instance, we know it can be pierced by radio waves.

From such a perspective, miracles no longer seem quite so miraculous. I mean, if piercing a wall is doable, what's to stop me from winning a date with that girl, or closing that contract?

The fact is, 150 years ago all kinds of things we take for granted now would have been regarded as black magic. Handheld machines that enable you to find any fact in seconds? Saying that to someone in 1850 might've gotten you institutionalized!

No way around it, if you're out there in the world, trying to make things happen, there are times you're going to lose. Accept that as a given.

But also know, since that's when your fear factor's probably going through the roof, that it's also when you've got to take special care to remember who you are and stay true to your best self. Because it is your unique human capital—equal parts positive values and hard-won perspective—that will bring you back.

The fact is, much as I regret certain mistakes, given who I am, I probably could not *not* have made them. Even now, for the life of me, I still don't get why it makes sense to walk into Starbucks and drop five bucks for a cup of coffee.

(And, by the way, as long as I'm confessing to a certain cultural illiteracy, I've also never gotten *Star Wars*.)

At the same time, it is my mix of personal attributes, quirks included, that has brought about my success. Indeed, resisting the (sometimes very strong) pressure to follow the crowd has often been especially rewarding.

And, even more so, in my entrepreneurial career, has been my conscious focus on my karmic credit score—in less grandiose terms, trying to do the right thing.

Sometimes it's painful. Probably the best business idea I ever had became one of my most devastating failures. It was a company called Physician Capital Group, a revolutionary billing system for doctors. I put together the team, raised a lot of money from others, and put in even more of my own. We were rocking and rolling, really starting to take off—and then came Obamacare. In combination with the lingering impact of the financial crisis, it was a bullet between the eyes. Since Obamacare cost hospitals between 27 and 37 cents of every dollar on Medicare patients, they canceled contracts left and right. Facing the reality that it would be prohibitively expensive to keep our technology current and try to hang on, I reluctantly pulled the plug.

As big a hit as I took personally, what most bothered me was the other investors, all of whom got involved because I'd asked them to. I'd given them a personal commitment that I was going to make this company a success, and the guilt I felt when it wasn't weighed on me tremendously. Under no contractual or other obligation to do so, I decided to refund some of what they'd invested out of my own pocket; enough that, with the tax write-off, they'd be at least close to whole.

What happened then? Think of it as karmic payback. Later, out of the blue, two deals fell in my lap, which together have enabled me to recover what I'd lost.

Things like that have happened over and over in my career. I can't say if we live multiple lifetimes, but I know for an absolute certainty that when I do the right thing in this one, I usually get paid back in spades—often many times over.

And when I screw up? The opposite—I get clobbered.

One of the advantages of having a mother who brought you into the world at eighteen is that, if you're lucky, she's still around longer than anyone else's mother. All the way to ninety, my Mom was as strong-willed and feisty as ever, and I loved her completely. Except for the one time she decided to sue someone and asked me to represent her. And, unfortunately, against my better judgment and every instinct, I agreed.

The case is one that never should have been filed. My mom's been to a chiropractor who she claims has hurt her neck. But the insurance company won't pay a dime, because her medical records are voluminous; she's been through a bunch of car accidents and has preexisting conditions up the wazoo. In short, the case is ridiculous. Now it's coming up for trial, and, naturally, Mom wants me to try it.

It's important to know that up to this point, I've never lost a civil case—fifty-one and zero, perfect record, undefeated. And while that's not necessarily as impressive as it might sound since, unlike in my criminal career, I generally only took civil cases I liked, that record was still a source of pride.

Well, I go into court and just get my ass kicked all over the place.

The worst part? As we're walking out of the courthouse, my Mom turns to my sister and says, "My son, the big shot trial lawyer, can't even win a case for his own mother!"

But I deserved it.

Mark that down as another lesson learned the hard way.

No question, karma also comes to play at least as powerfully in our personal lives. Indeed, in my own case the *greatest* failures have been on the personal side.

Maybe that was inevitable. Maybe emerging as I did from circumstances of insecurity and deprivation, my highest and almost exclusive priority *had* to be staking out a claim in the world large enough that I'd never again have to worry about being down and out. And maybe the focus essential to achieving that *had* to be so relentless it would crowd out my personal life. All I know is that I paid a steep price.

I recall an episode that made a particular impression on me back in the late 1980s. Bob Brown, a former close associate of Dr. King's, had invited me and a couple of other friends to accompany him to South Africa, where he had important business.

Bob is a remarkable man. Nixon recruited Bob to put real teeth in the Civil Rights Act. From the military to corporate America, he made sure qualified minorities were elevated to their rightful positions. I am extremely proud to say that Bob Brown and Maya Angelou were my sponsors into the Horatio Alger Association.

Bob was a close confidant of Martin Luther King Jr., who frequently used him to relay sensitive messages. At the time we met, Bob was performing the same function for the still-imprisoned Nelson Mandela in South Africa; he was acting as Mandela's go-between to P. W. Botha, the head of the country's apartheid regime. At the height of the secret negotiations, Bob invited me and two other close friends to join him on his latest visit to Johannesburg. When we arrived in South Africa, our little party was met at the airport by Winnie Mandela, and over the next few days we spent time at Winnie's home in Soweto and accompanied her into the worst townships—places white people never dared venture. We met with black ministers and white cabinet members, saw the notorious South African security forces close at hand, and also interacted with the Soweto Soccer Club, the black youths who'd later be identified as Winnie's personal hit squad.

Over two weeks, watching Bob move seamlessly between white and black worlds at dagger points, our little group naturally drew close. One of the other guys in particular interested me. About my age, tall, and with an easy, self-deprecatory manner, he was a successful businessman but seemed less obsessed with that side of his life than most I knew. In fact, recently engaged, he was as comfortable in his skin as anyone I'd encountered in a long time.

At the end of the trip, saying our good-byes at the airport, I shook his hand and asked him to please give my best to his fiancée, adding, "She sounds like a sweet girl."

I'll never forget the look that got from Bob Brown. "Don't you know who Stedman's fiancée is?" he asked incredulously, the moment we were alone.

"I have no idea."

"Oprah Winfrey!"

All these years later, Stedman and Oprah still haven't married, and I'm certainly not among those privy to the state of their relationship. Still, I'll never forget how dumbstruck I was that the man's easy self-confidence was so great it was untouched by his connection to one of the world's most powerful women. In two weeks he never mentioned her name although he spoke often and lovingly about his "fiancée." It was not a lack of ego, but an ego strong enough to be blithely indifferent to the world's opinion.

That wasn't me. I was totally consumed by my work and who I was working with. I drove myself relentlessly, and inevitably there were casualties.

Unquestionably, the greatest failure of my life, far worse than any business setback, was the end of my first marriage. It's easy to say it was no one's fault—I was twenty-one when we married, she was twenty-two, and (as is readily apparent to almost everyone except those doing it) at that age you usually have no idea yet who you are, let alone who the other person is. But that's not to say that I don't bear the primary responsibility—and that there weren't hard lessons to be learned.

When the end came, after thirty years, the squabbling over money and assets was needlessly ugly, and it obscured the good times, and the life-changing ones, that are part of every long-term relationship.

The truth is, we were badly mismatched from the start. She loved music, I'm tone deaf; I love sports, she couldn't care less; I'm passionate about current events, she barely followed the news. Given how little we had in common, it's amazing we stuck it out as long as we did.

Still, the experiences we shared were special, and still are, and I feel tremendous guilt for the unhappiness I brought her. She didn't deserve it. I was self-absorbed, impatient, hard driving, work obsessed; she just wanted to create a beautiful home and a life to go with it.

One incident says it all. I'm in the middle of a death-penalty murder case and don't make it home till around 10:30 p.m. Patti is waiting up for me, because she's picking new wallpaper for the kitchen and wants my opinion. So, I'm dead tired and have all this pressure from the trial—including the possibility of my client going to the gas chamber—and frankly I don't give a damn which floral pattern is prettier, which I'm sure is written all over my face. So just to get it done with, I point to one of the samples, but that's not good enough, she wants to know why. With that, I just blow up. "Can't you see I don't care?" I shout. "This is such stupid stuff!" And I stomp off into the bedroom, leaving her sitting there, in tears.

But it wasn't stupid stuff. Getting that kitchen right was a loving act on her part; she was a sweet, good person, and I was a total, narcissistic ass. And it broke her heart.

The only thing to be said on my behalf is that I have tried to learn from those experiences, transforming them after the fact into *positive* failures; and that I've learned along the way, painfully, how much richer life could be, if I'd let it.

Indeed, if my not making my first marriage work was the greatest failure of my life, professional or otherwise, my current marriage is by far my greatest success.

Kalli and I have *everything* in common, starting with the fact that she's a lawyer herself. She's incredibly verbal, is into current events, and is always up for a sharp exchange of ideas. In fact, she and Patti are such total opposites that I have to sit up and take serious notice when Kalli has the same complaints about me that Patti did; guess who is the common denominator.

The difference is, with Kalli there's no beating around the bush—I get it straight and she delivers it hard. Did I mention she spent some years as a prosecutor in the Houston district attorney's office and that she occasionally speaks the language of the criminal courts? I love that about her.

In Hollywood terms, Kalli and I met cute. We were on opposite sides of one of the most highly publicized court battles of its time, the three-way fight between Anna Nicole Smith, the voluptuous ex-Playboy Playmate widow of elderly billionaire J. Howard Marshall, and Marshall's two sons for control of Marshall's estate. There was an attraction when I first saw Kalli, and in court she was magnificent. But we did not date until my marriage finally imploded several months after the trial.

I really never thought I would remarry after Patti. But then Kalli came along, and she was so special. As Beyoncé advised, "If you like it, then you shoulda put a ring on it."

Well, "shoulda" is a word I hate. What it means to me is making the biggest mistake possible. "Shoulda" means I didn't act on it and now I have regret. I would much rather live with "shouldn't have" because then I at least tried and I don't have to wonder what would have happened. As Garth Brooks retorts, "I could have missed the pain, but I'da had to miss the dance." And I haven't missed a dance since the fourth grade!

There was just no way I was going to lose Kalli O'Malley. "Shoulda" was never going to be a part of our story. So, I "put a ring on it."

When Kalli and I married, almost a year after our date, it set me off on a whole new life. Kalli had children, ages eight and five at the time, meaning that for the first time, at fifty-four, on top of leaving California behind and relocating to Houston, I'm going to have kids in my life. Yet, there wasn't ten minutes' hesitation. What I'm thinking was: I'm going to *get* to do those things. We were going to make it work, and we did.

That was seventeen years ago, and I feel like Kalli and I are still on our honeymoon. She is drop-dead gorgeous, a great dancer, fun as hell. Sweet, smart, sassy, and sexy—the full package. But I really hadn't thought through what it means when you marry a woman with two young kids. I instantly inherited two kids, two dogs, and two *mothers-in-law*, since her ex-husband's mom wants to see and visit her grandkids. I guess it could have been a disaster, but it was just the opposite. Kalli's parents were fantastic, and Kalli and her ex were divorced for three years and Kevin had already remarried a great lady when I came along. She, like me, had no kids, and both of them are also lawyers. The four of us helped raise the kids with Kalli taking the lead. Kevin and Melanie became our good friends, and I love both my mothers-in-law, as well.

I have kept a list of things Kalli has said to me, which I refer to as Kallisms:

"You need to give love with no strings attached. Ropes maybe—but no strings."

"I am not too smart for my own good, I am too smart for your own good."

"Diamonds are not a girl's best friend, dimmers are."

"The only real power I have over you is sex—it's a doozie—but it's the only power."

How do you not fall in love with that?!

Kalli was an unbelievably gifted trial lawyer (win-loss record of 24–1) but she gave up her promising career for the kids and then me. She is as talented a person as I have ever met and would have been successful at anything she wanted to do. How lucky for me that being a great wife who supported my career while creating incredibly beautiful and art-filled environments for our family was high on her list of skill sets—and what she taught me about being a parent to Lauren and Keller I will never forget.

Childhood, for me, was a series of snapshots, some of them miserable, and I was intent on creating as few of those as possible. Nonetheless, we're all products of our own experience, and my instinctive answer to every time the kids said, "Why?" would have been: "Because I said so!" That would have been my go-to line, every time. But, as Kalli says, "Every time you say 'always' or 'every time'—you are 'always' wrong—'every time'."

In teaching me to treat children with the same respect I show adults, Kalli not only made me appreciate my incredible mom even more, she made me reflect on my own past, and especially my father, and to finally come to see him fully as he was, rather than through the hurt eyes of a child. I realized that he, too, probably had ADD, but without the compensating OCD, and was frustrated in every attempt to move forward. And while back then no one had heard of PTSD (and if anyone had, it would have been roundly dismissed as excuse making), he surely had a debilitating case of that, also. Read accounts of Saipan, as I now did, and the sheer hellishness of the experience comes through even on the page: the exploding shells on all sides as he steers his Higgins landing craft toward the beach, the floor festooned with the steak-and-eggs breakfasts of the terrified young marines; and then, after he's dropped open the craft's front and fire rakes the interior, with their blood.

There are faith systems that say we choose the environment we are born into, because there are things we need to learn, and sometimes our karmic table dictates the need for some pain. Who knows, maybe I picked my parents. My dad, *because* he wouldn't be around, so it forced me to rely on myself. My mom, to be my guardian angel. Someone who would instill positive thinking and self-confidence, while being lovingly tough enough to teach me to be a man.

Thinking about my dad that way enabled me to do my part in repairing our relationship over the last years of his life. If it could never be a classic father/son bond, we at least forged a friendship of equals.

I like to think I have put the pain of my childhood not just in the past, but in perspective. What I try to always keep front and center is this: All journeys begin within a moment of "now." Nothing is ever accomplished "later," "tomorrow," "next week," or "someday." "Now" is the only productive element of time. In any moment of "now," any of us can decide to wake up to the extraordinary power of who we really are. Most important, we can do so with positive thoughts of being our best self—or not. The choice is always ours.

CHAPTER THIRTEEN

Reflect, Regroup, Recharge

Everyone has the ability to be in the 15 percent

Everyone's life is a marathon, with plenty of steep hills, and there are times when sticking to the right path is itself a challenge. This is especially true for those of the 15 percent, who in their hard-charging rush forward can all but forget their original destination. It's vital to pause from time to time, take a breather, regroup, reflect. So, relax and lean back in your chair, because here comes my closing argument. (Sorry, but after all those years in the law I just can't help myself.)

I have focused on the traits, whether learned or inherent, that I believe help to create the 15 percent.

It starts with the development of a low fear factor, which builds confidence and the willingness to take smart risk. This allows life to expand outside the boundaries of your comfort zone, enriching and enlarging your universe of possibilities.

As Christopher Columbus supposedly said, "You can never cross the ocean until you have the courage to lose sight of the shore."

As a low fear factor expands what is possible, it simultaneously widens our view of ourselves and our true capabilities. We more fully understand our unique talents and skill sets so we can utilize capitalization learning and begin to see our future in new and exciting ways.

As you strengthen your ability to visualize your future and strengthen your conscious picture of what you want to be and do, you begin to develop underdog strategies that will allow you to break from the confinement of how others see you. You begin to do the unexpected, achieve what appear to others as astonishing results, and experience the first signs of true empowerment.

Now armed with the ability to clearly see the future you most desire, and the agility to get there, you must learn discipline to be careful about what you ask for. Unintended consequences can turn dreams into nightmares.

In essence, you have awakened within you the creative being you were intended to be. Having developed your power to focus your consciousness in tune with positive thinking, you learn to align your conversation with your vision. The power of words begins to turn your conscious vision into reality. ("A word fully spoken is like apples of gold in settings of silver," Proverbs 25:11.)

Having aligned your consciousness and your conversation, you now extend and sync your thinking and your words with your conduct. It is important to remain flexible and keep refining your current best idea of yourself until your consciousness, conversation, and conduct act as in singularity. You perfect the visualization of your dream and then make sure it is reinforced by everything you say and do.

Armed with all of the above in your personal toolbox, you are ready to excel and turn disadvantages into desirable disadvantages as opportunities begin to emerge in an endless bounty of possibilities.

Ralph Waldo Emerson said, "The only person you are destined to become is the person you decide to be." Why not decide to be the very best person you can envision?

I am of the absolute belief that we are creative beings. If you align your consciousness (mind), your conversation (words), and your conduct (actions), the Universe cannot deny you. The trilogy is now complete. Whether this is God creating us in his image, universal law, or some quantum physics phenomenon—I believe it is the truth.

However, if life dishes out major disadvantages (losing one or both parents, sexual abuse, major physical handicaps), it can very well, and understandably, appear as if life were something that happens to you.

But if you, by design or by accident, develop a low fear factor (take smart risks), use and develop your God-given talents (capitalization learning), and develop the ability to do and accomplish the unexpected (underdog strategies), you realize that you can turn disadvantages into assets that make you tougher, smarter, and more resilient than you ever imagined. In short, you realize that life is something you create for yourself. As you get better at visualization and learn to align everything you say and do with that vision, nothing seems impossible.

Some years ago, Adidas ran an ad that said it all:

"Impossible is just a big word thrown around by small men who find it easier to live in the world they've been given than to explore the power they have to change it. Impossible is not a fact. It's an opinion. Impossible is not a declaration. It is a dare. Impossible is potential. Impossible is temporary. Impossible is nothing."

Knowingly or unknowingly, the 15 percent dial into this strategy on a constant basis.

The question then becomes, why is it that only 15 percent make the transformation? If we understand the traits that help to define the 15 percent, what are the traits that act as a barrier to entrance into this select group?

There is no question society needs the 15 percent. They make things work, provide jobs, create the economy, and pay most of the taxes. Whether we like it or not, society must be organized. There must be laws. New and better products must be developed. To use an old euphemism—the trains have to run on time. But what is it that seems to limit transformation to just 15 percent?

I am afraid that I cannot definitively answer that question. But here is the scary truth. As creative beings, we are all creating our lives. We are doing it consciously with purpose or unconsciously with no purpose or direction. If positive thinking works, so does negative thinking. You become the person you think you are.

The world is full of naysayers and those who will fill your head with negatives about who you are and who you will become. In addition, there are real mental obstacles that emerge as a result of being born poor or handicapped or abused in some way. The path to success can seem nonexistent.

By some unexplained phenomena, 15 percent are able to adapt by using the techniques I have described to rise above the chaos of disadvantage, while 85 percent fall under the hypnotic drone of victimhood in one form or another. Are these percentages written into the physical world's DNA as part of nature's plan pursuant to "survival of the fittest"? Or is it up to the human race, as a sentient species of spiritual faith, to elevate the soul of the collective to a true understanding of their God-given creative ability?

I do not pretend to know the answer to those questions, but if I am wrong, I have decided to err on the side of spiritual faith and the elevation of the collective soul.

I am also confident in my belief that the way things are is not the way things have to be. What I am clear about is that our mind is the key. How we think is who we become. Thoughts are energy and the first building block of bringing things into reality. Therefore, remaining positive, not giving in to victimhood, and constantly making your life and business better by improving on your current best idea is rational, the recipe for true self-fulfillment, and the mantra for the 15 percent. Being negative and giving in to victimhood carry no rewards nor do they allow for self-improvement. There is no logic that changes that fact. Lewis Carroll, writing about Wonderland in *Through the Looking-Glass,* puts the following immortal words into the mouth of Tweedledee:

"If it was so, it might be; and if it were so, it would be; but as it isn't, it ain't. That's logic."

What's worse, victimhood exists not just in singular incidents. Whole cultures have been built around it, with the leaders gaining fame and fortune by teaching their followers, not that they can stand on their own two feet and take back the power of their creative selves, but that they are victims of the past, present, and future. Sadly, they can infect the minds and the thoughts of an entire nation. The consciousness is one of victimhood, the conversations are those of victimhood, the conduct is that of a victim. Little wonder such a culture will struggle to escape the trap of their own making. In those communities there must be a renewal, a rethinking that will use the disadvantages of the past to develop the strength to become their true selves—creative beings.

Pascal's Wager argues that belief makes more sense than disbelief when the worst outcome is a total loss. If so, supporting a shift in consciousness from one of victimhood to one of self-fulfillment makes sense, especially when every psychiatrist worth their salt will admit that being stuck in a victim mentality is a sure road to negativity and the destruction of healthy self-worth.

Ultimately, each of us controls his own destiny. We just have to learn to live life with intention, on purpose, fully conscious and awake. As quoted in Ephesians 4:23—"Be made new in the attitude of your mind." In very real ways, life *is* mind over matter.

The 15 percent is real, and I am hopeful that the 15 percent will someday be the 25 percent, or the 50 percent, or even more. The world needs fearless men and women who confront the status quo, continually re-creating themselves and the world around them. Those who can and will move the collective soul of the human race to a higher level.

One last thought—or maybe a mild warning. Have a powerful and positive vision of the best "you" you can imagine, align your behavior and your words with your beliefs, have the guts to follow through, see to it that all setbacks are temporary—and most people will say you're just lucky.

Let them think that. Work hard, and there's always someone who thinks they can outwork you. Be smart, and there's always someone who believes he is smarter. Bring capital, and there's always someone who has more money. Be tough, and there's always someone who thinks they are tougher. But be lucky, and people no longer even mind losing to you. They just walk away, head shaking, and mumbling to themselves— "You just can't beat lucky."

Acknowledgments

I want to acknowledge my wife, Kalli O'Malley, who has sacrificed her own fantastic career as a trial lawyer to support me and our children. Without her, not even this book would have been possible. I am very grateful for the excellent assistance of Harry Stein's creative guidance and leadership in helping to create *The Fifteen Percent*, as well as his friendship. The folks at Skyhorse Publishing, Tony Lyons and Rebecca Shoenthal, have been incredible in their support and confidence in this project. Tony is not only a publisher, but he has the heart of a true entrepreneur. Kristen Blackford, my chief of staff for thirty years is my right (and left) arm, and I could not run my life without her. I am extremely grateful for my friends who took the time to read the drafts of *The Fifteen Percent* and gave me their honest input. Nothing seems to happen in this world without proper marketing, and the wizardry of Armstrong Williams was invaluable. Finally, thank you to all of you who have allowed me into your world so that I might learn the lessons recorded here. That includes my clients, my business partners, my friends, my enemies, and all those who touched my personal life. Each of you impacted and educated me, and I am grateful for the time we spent together regardless of how or why. To those I may have hurt or offended, I apologize. To those I may have helped or influenced, thank you for allowing me to grow through my relationship with you. I am the final product of all that I have experienced, and those experiences have influenced the decisions I have made along the way—some good and some not so good. The good I owe to all of you out there with whom I have had contact. The not-so-good—that's on me!